Exploring
the Norfolk Village

Christopher Barringer

POPPYLAND
PUBLISHING

First published 2005
ISBN 0 946148 71 6

Published by Poppyland Publishing, Cromer, NR27 9AN

Picture credits
Hethersett Village Archive: page 142
Poppyland Photos: pages 129, 132, 133, 136, 137, 140, 141

Unless otherwise stated in the captions, all other maps and diagrams have been drafted by the author and redrawn by Ruth Murray. All black and white photographs are by the author.

The maps on pages 15, 29 and 57 are based on Ordnance Survey mapping, reproduced by permission of Ordnance Survey on behalf of HMSO © Crown copyright 2005. All rights reserved. Ordnance Survey Licence number 100044755.

Designed and typeset in 9½ on 12 pt Arial by Watermark, Cromer, NR27 9HL

Printed by Printing Services (Norwich) Ltd

NORFOLK ORIGINS 8

EXPLORING THE NORFOLK VILLAGE

Further details on these titles can be found at
www.poppyland.co.uk
where clicking on the 'Support and Resources' button
will lead to pages specially compiled to support this title.

A DVD Exploring the Norfolk Village *is also available*
in association with this book, introduced by Christopher Barringer and
offering supplementary materials to those interested in exploring further.
For further details consult www.poppyland.co.uk

Preface

As is only too clear from the Contents page, this is not an attempt to look at all Norfolk's villages. When I came to Norfolk from Lancashire, I had to adjust to this spacious, rural county, and I became aware of its sub-regions; the first part of this book attempts to show how their differences influence the activity of man to a greater or lesser extent. Norfolk is an old county and phase after phase of human development has left its mark on it; the second group of chapters aims to illustrate some of these phases and their impact on what we now see.

After living and working in Norfolk for 40 years I have had the privilege of getting to know the county as part of my work as a tutor in local and regional history. As a resident tutor for Cambridge University Board of Extra-Mural Studies, and later as Director of the Centre for Continuing Education at the University of East Anglia (UEA), I had the good fortune to work with adult groups all over the county. Several of the studies in this book stem from research carried out when preparing for classes from Hunstanton to Harleston. I have gradually acquired a mass of material about Norfolk's villages and market towns. Over the years I have been lucky to explore many of these with David Yaxley, Alan Davison and David Dymond and I have learnt much from all of them. Field work with the former Research Committee (now the Norfolk Archaeological and Historical Research Group) and the Norfolk and Norwich Archaeology Society have again added to my experience.

I was closely associated with the Centre of East Anglian Studies at the UEA, where I was welcomed by successive staff there – the late Alan

Carter, Professor Hassell Smith, Dr Tom Williamson and others. In 1975 *East Anglian Archaeology* began an invaluable series, 104 volumes to date, on the archaeology and landscape history of East Anglia. I have had the good fortune to meet many of the archaeologists and related researchers of this series by being a member of the Scole Committee. Since arriving in Norfolk I have made much use of the Norfolk Record Office and the Local Studies Library (now the Heritage Centre) and I am grateful to the staffs of both for their friendliness and help.

Without the encouragement of Peter Stibbons of Poppyland Publishing and of my wife Charlotte who has dealt with modern technology for me, this book would not have been written. My thanks also to Ruth Murray for her maps.

Maps and photographs do not mean that public access is available to sites included in this study.

Contents

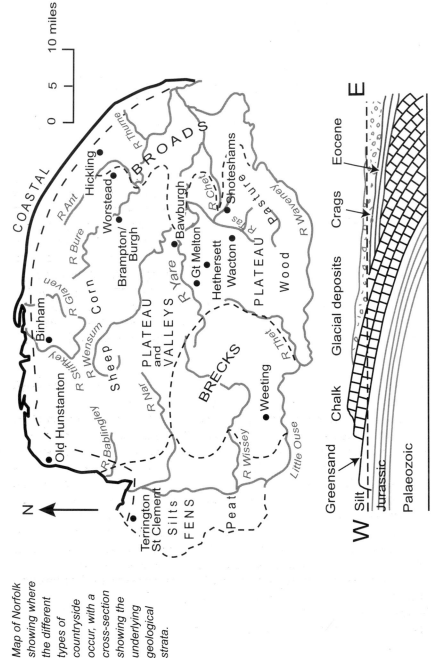

Map of Norfolk showing where the different types of countryside occur, with a cross-section showing the underlying geological strata.

N

0 5 10 miles

COASTAL

BROADS

R Thurne

Hickling

R Ant

Worstead

R Bure

Brampton/
Burgh

R Glaven

Corn

Sheep

R Wensum

Binham

R Stiffkey

Old Hunstanton

R Bablingley

R Nar

PLATEAU
and
VALLEYS

R Yare

Gt Melton

Hethersett

Wacton

Bawburgh

R Chet

R Tas

Shoteshams

PLATEAU

Wood

Pasture

R Waveney

BRECKS

R Thet

Weeting

R Wissey

Little Ouse

Peat

FENS

Silts

Terrington
St Clement

W

Greensand

Chalk

Glacial deposits

Crags

Eocene

E

Silt

Jurassic

Palaeozoic

INTRODUCTION

Norfolk, according to Noel Coward, is very flat. To those who get to know the county, it soon becomes clear that not all Norfolk is flat – in Sheringham Park, for example, or when climbing Gas Hill in Norwich. In fact, Norfolk consists of a number of very different countrysides, what the French term *pays*. These countrysides have subtle but distinctive characteristics – the sandy soils and pine trees of the Breck, the drainage dykes of the Fens, the marshes and open water of the Broads, the varied forms of coastline, the shallow but distinctive river valleys and finally the areas of plateau where church towers, high trees and electricity pylons provide the skyline. The diagrams or models try to bring out some of the characteristics of the *pays,* as do the photographs.

Underneath the varied surface soils lies a 'raft' of chalk which tilts eastwards under the North Sea so that layers of chalk well above sea level at Hunstanton are deep below glacial deposits at Yarmouth. The chalk is extremely significant in that it holds water, it consists of calcium carbonate (lime) and it contains, in increasing quantities from west to east, layers of flint. The lime is a valuable influence in soil quality and in places the chalk can be used for building (clunch). The flint is almost a symbol of Norfolk for its impact on the buildings of the county. Over the chalk, extending as far west as Hingham, the various shelly, shallow sea crags were deposited between two million and half a million years ago. Over nearly the whole of the county a chaotic mixture of debris was left by glaciers during the quaternary glaciations. These deposits range from boulder clays over much of the plateau to sand, gravel and heaps of boulders elsewhere. One has only to stand on the former sand dunes at Wangford Warren near Brandon, in Suffolk, and compare them with a wet field of boulder clay near Wacton to appreciate the difference. Yet these deposits are localised.

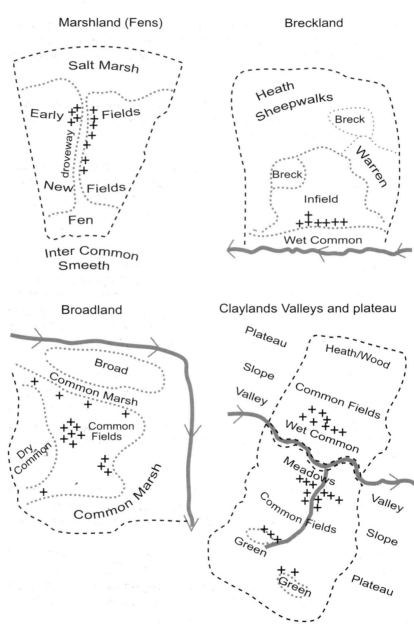

*Some characteristic village patterns
in the regions of Norfolk.*

The Norwich–Holt road more or less follows a boundary between glacial soils so that to its east Horsford, Hevingham, Marsham and Cawston have heaths and warrens but to its west Cawston and other villages have arable land.

To the west of the chalk, and geologically beneath it, lies a narrow zone of carstone (greensand in name but orangey brown to look at). This provides a distinctive building stone, of which more later.

Further west again is a quite different zone – the fenland. This has two types of soils: near to the sea, silts have accumulated; further inland, where landwater could not easily escape to the sea, peats developed where the plant cover fell into standing water and no oxygen could help to decay the plant remains.

Switching to the east of the county, the infilling of river estuaries led to silts and peats filling in former deep valley floors. The streams coming off the plateau, bringing lime-rich water from the chalky boulder clay, enabled a wide range of plants to flourish and under natural conditions peaty alder carr gave way to sea-washed salt marshes. Man has however altered all this by digging for peat and embanking the slow-flowing rivers.

The rivers provide a final and very attractive element in the Norfolk landscape. Their valleys, now shallow but deeper in glacial times, are being filled in by slow-flowing rivers. The valley of the Wensum provides striking views as it opens out upstream from Norwich. Meadows, grazing cattle and watermills give a landscape loved by the Norwich School of painters and further south in Suffolk by John Constable.

The subtleties of the surface of Norfolk help to explain some of the differences between the evolution and economy of some of the county's villages and those considered to typify the differences are shown in the diagrams.

Man has, however, affected the way in which these regions have been used for the last ten thousand years. From the time when Mesolithic man, with his flint tools, began to hunt animals and burn vegetation the natural plant cover began to be affected. The ultimate impact of man, now being debated because of increasing awareness of his effect on the physical environment, is to be seen in the debates on the dualling of our main roads, the protection of our coastline and the extension of urban areas. Later chapters in this study aim to show how different phases of human activity have used and affected the physical landscape and how they have helped to create the complex landscape of Norfolk as we now see it.

The length and scale of this book and the author's particular interests will condition the way in which the human part of this story is told. So, however, will the fact that it is Norfolk which is the theme of the book. Monasteries have been more significant to Norfolk's history than they have, let us say, in North Wales. The evolution of agriculture has dominated the story when compared with the coalfield areas of England. Change has been, perhaps until now, less dramatic than in the semi-urbanised regions of Surrey. Agriculture has been linked to great estates, especially in the west of the county. The sea, as physical force for change, as a source of prosperity and as a means of cultural contact with north-west Europe, has had a great influence.

Despite a conscious effort to give less emphasis to the parish church than is given in many texts on Norfolk, the significance of the church in the creation of the character of many of the villages has to be admitted. I call them villages, for although many of the smaller settlements discussed did at some time have markets, none would now be considered a market town. We can visualise the villages of the county as having evolved through a sequence of rather arbitrary phases. The fascination is the extent to which these phases exert particular influences in particular cases.

The Regions of Norfolk

The coast: *Hunstanton*

What is now known as Old Hunstanton lies at the north-western limit of the county. It is a parish where land and sea meet but with a different balance from that of Terrington St Clement. The land is higher, for this is where the western edge of the chalk raft of Norfolk is exposed in the distinctive cliffs where not only the chalk but the red chalk below it and the carstone below that is exposed. Over the chalk lies a veneer of glacial debris but it is thin compared with the depths of boulder clay that cover central Norfolk. Compared with Terrington, the sea here is an eroding agent at the foot of the cliffs, not one piling up silts against sea walls. However, to the north of the cliffs the sand dunes have built up. The chalk is usable as 'clunch' for building and provides a pleasant variation in the appearance of buildings in the area. It is also near enough the surface to provide grazings for sheep; at Ringstead Downs there is even a stretch of real downland landscape. The carstone provides the orangey brown, rather crumbly sandstone that gives a distinctive colour to the buildings of a narrow band of country from Hunstanton southwards, place-names such as Sandringham and Sandy (in Bedfordshire) providing a clue to its outcrop.

Hunstanton beach at low tide: carstone cut into pillars by the waves of the sea.

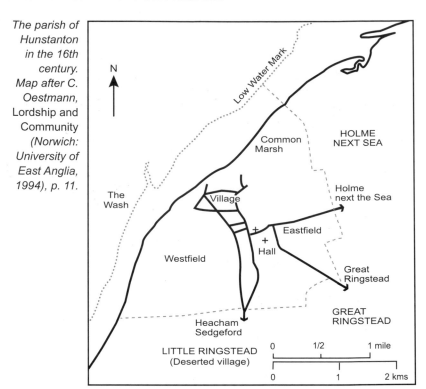

The parish of Hunstanton in the 16th century. Map after C. Oestmann, Lordship and Community (Norwich: University of East Anglia, 1994), p. 11.

The parish of Hunstanton formed a triangle of land. In the 16th century the hall lay between an East Field and a West Field. The East Field gradually diminished as the Le Strange family increased the size of their park.

Hunstanton lies near to the point where the Icknield Way and the Peddars Way virtually join. Luton Brain suggested that the Icknield Way reached the sea in Hunstanton and the Peddars Way in Holm.[1] He listed the then known archaeological sites which included Neolithic, Bronze Age, Roman, an Early Saxon inhumation cemetery and later Saxon and Medieval finds. The map opposite shows how rich in Romano-British finds this area was by 1986, Snettisham holding pride of place as the site of the Iron Age treasure.[2] Most recently another Iron Age site, just to the south of New Hunstanton, has been published by John Wymer.[3] No distance away, at Holme-next-Sea, came the remarkable find of Seahenge in 2000. This is now known to be a Bronze Age site consisting of a circle of timber posts with a huge upturned timber in the centre. The timbers from this circle, despite much debate, were lifted and are in 2003 being conserved at Flag

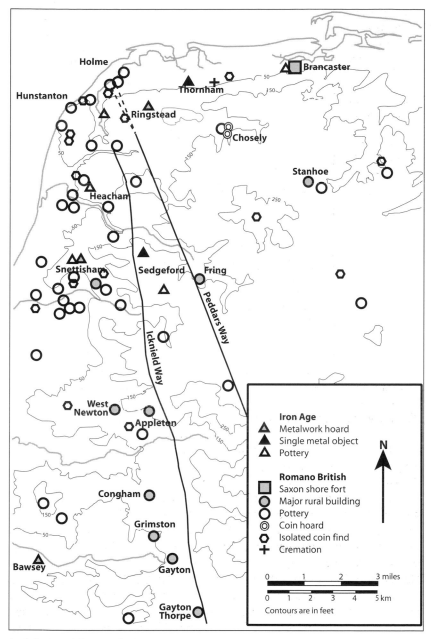

Iron Age and Roman finds in north-west Norfolk, after T. Gregory and D. Gurney's map in East Anglian Archaeology *30 (1986), p.2.*

Fen near Peterborough. In brief, man has been around in the area during many of the recognised phases of his cultural development.

Hunstanton in Domesday Book

The first documentary evidence of holdings in this part of Norfolk is to be found in one of the very few Anglo-Saxon charters that survive for the county: 'AD 1035–40. The will of Aelfric Bishop included bequests of land at . . . Hunstanton, Holme, Tichwell and Docking, Norfolk, to Bury St Edmunds'.[4]

Domesday Book, produced in 1086, tells us that by 1066 Stigand, the Archbishop of Canterbury, held a part of the vill. He lost his lands to William I and the King held them in 1086. Roger Bigot, Earl of Norfolk from 1077, was given another part of the vill which had formerly been held by a freeman. John Nephew of Waleran, another Norman, held a third portion of the vill. In addition several freemen attached to these holdings also held land.

How do we interpret this complicated entry? Were there three separate little settlements, each with its cluster of crofts around a hall, each with its own lands, or was the vill split into three by arbitrary agreement perhaps in pre-Conquest time? A church lay in Waleran's holding; Roger Bigot, Waleran and two freemen each held a fishery and the King had half a fishery. There was a total of 74 heads of households in the Domesday entry and this might represent about 300 people in Hunstanton in 1086; in 1841 there were 527.

Hunstanton and the sea

The cliffs, shore and marshes all played a part in the influence of the sea on Hunstanton. A remarkable series of bailiffs' account books for the Le Strange manors has survived; one such set covers 1605 to 1626.[5] Most of the accounts are concerned with rental income and various expenses; amongst the expenses the following records appear:

> 1606   1 ramotge falcon capt apud le Cliffe December 12
> 1607   1 ramotge falcon capt apud le Cliffe October 20
>   1 ramotge falcon capt idem 28 November
>   1 ramotge falcon of one [?] tiercelett capt idem 11 [illegible]

A 'ramotge' falcon is given in the *Oxford English Dictionary* as a ramage, which is a hawk that has left the nest and has begun to fly from branch to branch. A tiercelett was the male of any kind of hawk, but especially of a peregrine. The bailiff recorded £2 against one of these entries – the Le Stranges were prepared to pay well for additions to their falconry. In the early 17th century Hunstanton cliffs must have had a number of peregrine nests on the ledges.

Below and beyond the cliffs was a complicated series of fishing rights which were described in great detail for 1616 when they were renewed.[6] It seems that these rights, known as 'lawers in the sea', went originally with tenements held from the manor. In this way most Hunstanton tenants had a right to some fishing. Cord Oestmann notes that no good description of the physical rights existed but he quotes a document of 1606 which gives some idea. He says that the lawers stretched in about 30 rows, from east to west, from shore to sea from the north end of the cliffs towards Holme-next-the-Sea. Some rows contained 26 'pokenets', others as many as 180.[7] A brief extract from the 1616 document shows that in row 1 Thomas Page had 36 pokenets and further out 12 pokenets. In row 2 Edmund Cremer and Roger Pedder had 26, Roger Browne and James Browne 26, Edmund Cremer and John Pedder 26 and Edmund Cremer and William Pedder 24.

This pattern describes 30 rows. The same tenants' names occur frequently. Oestmann suggests that by the 17th century some of the tenants, as with landholdings, were buying out others and so accumulating more pokenet sites. There was also oyster gathering on an area known as the 'scarpe' and boats fishing that area made payments to the Le Stranges.[8] The accounts of Hamon Le Strange for 1610 refer to Lynn men receiving food on 5th May when 'they came about fishing'.

Hunstanton: the Le Strange family and the estate

Norfolk is a county of large estates and this corner is occupied by one of the oldest: that of the Le Strange family based at Hunstanton Hall. Walter Rye, one of Norfolk's great late-19th-century historians, says 'the family is the oldest in the county to retain property held in the female line practically from the conquest'.

Sir Hamon L'Estrange who died in 1317 was probably the first member of the family to live at Hunstanton. Thereafter a remarkable continuity ran through until the present day. As in so many of the Norfolk landed families, the L'Estranges intermarried with many of the other gentry families; for example, Drury, Heydon, Knivett, Hastings, Yelverton and Coke, among others. Rye points out that there were even three L'Estrange brothers at Agincourt in 1415 and that Sir Thomas was at the Field of the Cloth of Gold with Henry VIII in 1520. In 1629 Sir Hamon L'Estrange was made a baronet and he was followed by six more baronets until the baronetcy ceased in 1762. In the late 18th century a daughter, Armine L'Estrange, married a Styleman and the Styleman name continued until the 1860s when Le Strange (note the spelling) was used as the family name again.

The advantage, to an historian, of studying a village such as Hunstanton is that having been in the hands of a single family, the Le Stranges, there is a likelihood of the accumulation of family papers over the centuries. This is indeed the case and in the Norfolk Record Office a calendar of the Le Strange papers reveals the wealth of documents that has accumulated. Hamon Le Strange, who was High Sheriff in 1609 and MP for Castle Rising in 1625 and who died in 1654,[9] left a series of beautifully kept account books of which one page is quoted for 27th July to 4th August 1610.[10]

July 27th	Given to a boy that brought aprecokts from Joseph Walker 6d.
28	To Mr Nickolls for his paynes & physick for Nick £2 10s.
30	Given to a boy that brought salmon from Bloy 6d.
31	For drawing two caps for Mr Strange 4d.
31	For 3lb of corants and 3lb of reysons 3s 0d.
31	For oyle of dill and oyle of cammamoyle 1s 0d.
31	For 2 yards and a quarter of cushion canviss 3s 0d.
31	For half a pound of Crewells 2s 9d.
31	Given to Salter for going to Norwich 2s 0d.
Aug 2nd	Given to Harryson's boy for bringing mead 4d.
2	To a boy that brought pease from Edward Spratt 3d.
3	Paid for a porkpiss [porpoise?] 2s 0d.
4	For a hatt band 5s.
4	For a dozen of points 2s 6d.
4	For a yard of riband 6d.
4	For paper 2d.
4	For the Ecclesiasticall Cannon 1s 4d.
4	For two haukes hoods 2s 0d.
4	For a combe 8d.
4	For wall fringes 2s 0d.

4	For 3 glasse cruetts 1s 6d.
4	Paid for a marchpane which was given to Sir Thomas, Barny 13s 4d.
4	Paid to Jeffreys upon his bill 2s 0d.
4	Paid to Anguish for 5 yardes and a half of striped say 14s 8d.
4	To Sappe for a payer of russet bootes 10s 0d.
4	For new footing of a payer of bootes 3s 0d.
4	Given to one for a hatt bringing from London to Mr Strange 4s 6d.
4	For bringing a lode of charcole 2s 0d.
4	For a payer of gloves for Mr Strange 1s 4d.
4	For a pound of glue 6d.
4	To my Cosen Willyam Strange his mayd for bringing peaches 6d.
4	To a boy for bringing ducklings from Thornham 4d.
4	To the carters for bringing timber from Gressenhall to Rougham 10d.
4	To Mason for going to Well for horses 1s 6d.
4	To Edmund Skrimes boy for bringing pigeons 6d.

This set of accounts, covering a fortnight, throws a fascinating light on costume, diet and a variety of purchases for a major Norfolk gentry household. Mr Strange's clothes were a big item; summer fruits such as apricots and peaches were grown locally. Salmon was eaten. Was the porpoise brought to the Le Stranges because of their shore rights? Two hawks' hoods were provided for their falcons. Journeys to and from Norwich, London and Well (Upwell or Outwell) emphasise the range of contacts such a household had. These accounts are only a fraction of those for 1610 which run to 20 pages of transcripts.

The wages paid to members of the household varied from Robert Brutton's £8 8s to others being paid £2. Some were paid by the quarter, for example, Jaques Lane received £3 3s 4d. There were six household staff in all. Many others occur on a regular basis for payment for working on the land and buildings: on 3rd April Breeze was paid 3s 4d for threshing and dressing a combe of oats, presumably for the horses.

The chapman appeared to call every so often and a burst of expenditure was then made upon haberdashery, for example, 'three dozen and a half of silk buttons 1s 6d . . . nine yards of perpetuana at 4s 4d for a suit for Mr Strange'.[11]

The role of the Le Stranges, as rectors of both Hunstanton and Holme churches, is revealed. In May 1610 Thomas and James Horne were paid for 14 days' work about the chancel at a cost of 11s 8d. On 15th June Gray, the glazier, provided 78 feet of glass for the chancel and 140 quarrells for various windows in the chancel at 1d the quarrell totalling 11s 8d. On 7th and 8th July James Horne was paid for work at Holme mending the tower windows and whiting the chancel. Poor rates had to be paid and Mr Le Strange also gave money to poor individuals on several occasions.

The farming year can be followed. On 2nd June, Biders was paid for two days' mowing and on 16th Robinson was paid for three days' mowing grass. Dykes were dug and a pond created in the park. On 2nd July Jolles was paid

Below: *Chalk, red chalk and carstone in Hunstanton cliffs. The same three substances are seen used as building materials in the gable ends of the Le Strange Arms* (above left) *and a cottage near St Mary's church* (above right).

Hunstanton Hall

4s for felling timber. By 19th July hay was being made and by 2nd August peas were being brought from Edward Spratt. By 19th August money was paid to harvest men and by the 31st filberts came from Mrs Bayton.

Finally, two fascinating references appear which help to explain how the Le Strange manuscripts include a number of very fine maps. In April £1 1s 4d was paid for three 'mappe frames' and £2 1s 6d was paid 'for a geodetical staff and the boxe to put it in'. Then on 26th June £5 was 'payd for a brasse instrument called a theodolitt'. This was state of the art surveying equipment for use perhaps by those who made the Hunstanton maps. Perhaps one day an enthusiast for the study of a major household will transcribe the whole of this volume, which is the first of several.

The cliffed section of the Hunstanton coastline, revealing the unique geological sequence of carstone, red chalk and chalk helps to explain the character of many of the buildings of old Hunstanton. The Hall itself, especially the imposing gatehouse of 1487 set inside the moat, uses a rather different pattern, one of brick solely for the gatehouse and of flint and carstone chequers on the outside of the surviving courtyard ranges and carstone solely on the inside. Viewed from the west across the widened moat, the whole group of earlier remnants and later additions forms a striking picture. When New Hunstanton was built, block carstone was used for the façades of buildings but rubble carstone for the less visible parts. Sadly, the late medieval and Tudor parts of the Hall were badly damaged in fires of 1853 and 1947.

A separate account, kept in 1610, shows the great care with which building work was undertaken.[12] Some extracts are shown below:

A note what I have dispersed to masons, carpenters and other labourers in building the deyrey and altering the brewhouse and for brick, tile, lath, hayre, nayls and other necessaries and the charge of making the lime keele and coles to burn within

Given to Horn the mason for his travall and drawinge the platte of the house 4s.

More to Voyce in part payment for the lime keele 13s.

To a labourer for two days and a half in taking brick out of the old chimbney for the lime keele 2s 1d.

Paid to Voyce in full satisfaction for making the lime keele 15s.

For 7,000 of brick at 12s the thousand £4 4s.

For carriage of 7,000 brick from Stow [Stow Bardolph, where the Hare family had major brickworks] to Hunstanton £1 8s.

To the lime burner for burning 28 chalder of lime at 9d the chalder £1 1s.

To Bidden for 20 days breaking stone [chalk] for the lime keele 6s 8d.

For 16,000 tile at 11s 6d the thousand £9 4s.

Hunstanton Hall was built about 1500 by Sir Roger Le Strange, whose brass of 1506 is in St Mary's church. The east front (shown here (in a drawing from the Norfolk Record Office, MS 21219) as it was before the fire of 1853) was altered in 1835–6 by Henry L'Estrange Styleman Le Strange; he also added to the park and closed the old public roads running through it.

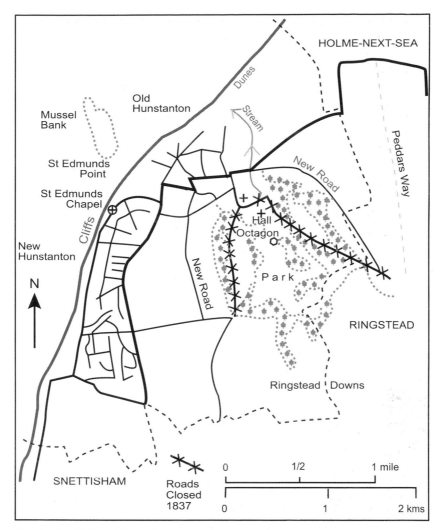

Hunstanton Hall and its park.

For 400 paving tile £2.

Payd to Thomas Horne according to his agreement at 12*d* the foot square for half the house which is 58 foote in length and 12 foote and a half in heighth from the levell ground upward into which bargaine he tileth and paveth and casteth the walls and partitions £36 5*s*.

To my father for boarding the lime burner and one to digge him stone four weekes and three dayes at 3*s* 4*d* a week eyther of them £1 10*s*.

The total cost of this operation was £124 12*s* 1*d*. The care with which these accounts of 1610 were drawn up reflects the sophisticated level of estate accounting at Hunstanton.

The park in which the Hall lies originated as a medieval deer park which was gradually extended. Bryant's map of 1826 shows it as roughly triangular with the Hall and gardens at the northern apex. An extension to the south was added between 1859 and 1906 so that it just touches Ringstead Downs. In the style of most large estates a boundary barrier of woodland separates it from the outside world. Within the park various ornamental features and additional plantations have been added by successive Le Stranges and Stylemans.

The Le Stranges owned land in an arc of villages around Hunstanton. The chalk soils drained well and gave good pasture so that the famous Norfolk combination of sheep and barley formed the main base of the economy. In the 16th and 17th centuries, because of the demand for wool for the worsted and broadcloth industries, sheep were a valuable product and in the 1530s Sir Thomas Le Strange had nine flocks spread across his manors; by 1543 he had 2,860 sheep. Sheep had another important role: their dung kept the arable land fertile, and in the 1530s barley was the dominant crop, grown on 72% of the land that was cropped. Edmund Spencer, one of Sir Thomas's tenants, left a long and fascinating will.[13] In it he left bushels of barley to the religious gilds in Hunstanton's church and to pay for altar candles there. The barley was sold to make malt for brewing and much of it would have been carted to Lynn for shipping to London or perhaps shipped direct from Hunstanton.

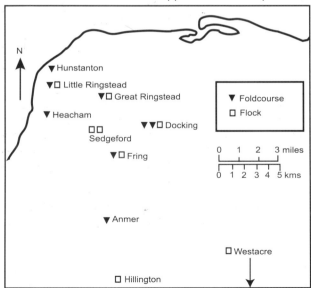

The L'Estrange family's foldcourses and flocks between 1520 and 1547 (based on Oestmann, map 4).

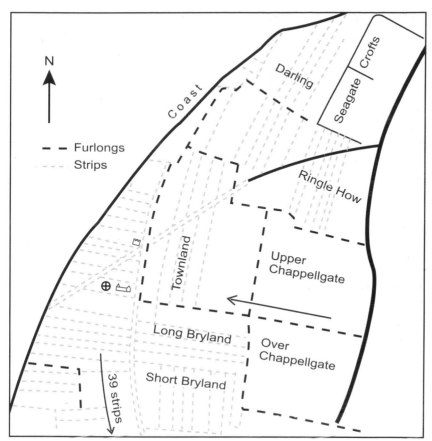

A little bit of Hunstanton's West Field as it was in 1689 when the arable land still lay in many strips. The coastline may well have changed: St Edmund's Chapel is clearly marked, further from the sea than it is now. Since this date the strips have been merged into larger units but the lines of trackways and boundaries often survive. Much of the southern half of the area shown on this map is now largely covered by New Hunstanton. (After a field book now in the Norfolk Record Office [LEST BH9].)

Outside the park lay the more traditionally farmed areas of the manor. Two large medieval open arable fields, the West Field and the East Field, lay either side of the park.

In 1845 Henry Le Strange decided to build a carefully planned, socially select new town in his parish. It was to be built 'with the view to meeting the express desire of many families in Norfolk and neighbouring counties to have the opportunity of enjoying the advantages of sea air and prospects'.

The detached cottages were to cost between £700 and £800, and this price would have made them exclusive. The young William Butterfield was engaged in 1845 by H. L. Styleman Le Strange to design the layout of the proposed town.[14] In a letter to Mr Bulwer (presumably of Heydon Hall) Le Strange says that Butterfield 'is delighted with the idea of having a place to build de Novo, we propose to have it all in the Old English style'. So began a new town entirely on Le Strange land. The very neat original plan centred on a village green was somewhat unbalanced by the arrival of the railway in 1862 between the green and the sea and several terraces replace the original detached cottages.

Hunstanton has much in it still that survives from past centuries – the coast, part of the fabric of the Hall, the park, the old village and many of its lanes and field boundaries. Yet out of the initiative of its main landowner a completely new element, New Hunstanton, also contributes to what is now to be seen there.

Fen and coast: *The Terringtons*

The Terringtons stretch for nine and a half miles from the southern marshes of The Wash southwards across the siltlands of marshland to the peaty soils of the Smeeth. They form one segment of an arc of parishes which stretches from Walsoken to Clenchwarton. Their history is one of a complex interplay between sea water and fresh water. Unlike the north-east

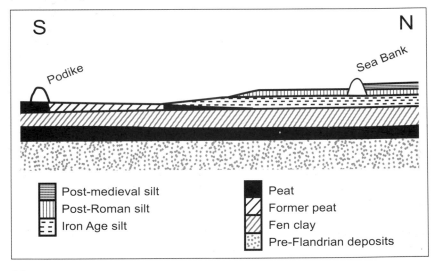

S   N

Podike   Sea Bank

▤ Post-medieval silt	◼ Peat
▥ Post-Roman silt	▨ Former peat
⊡ Iron Age silt	▧ Fen clay
	⊡ Pre-Flandrian deposits

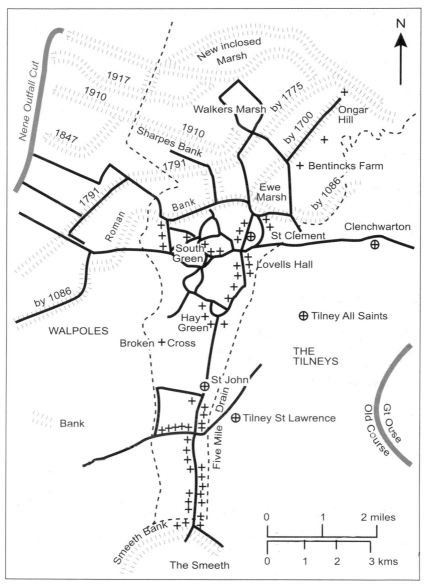

Above: *A diagrammatic map of the Terrington area, showing the parishes of St Clement and St John.*

Opposite: *Schematic section (by R. J. Silvester) through the Flandrian deposits in marshland (from* East Anglian Archaeology 45 (1988), fig. 5).

27

Terrington St Clement parish church, the 'Cathedral of the Fens'.

coast of Norfolk, the land here has gained overall yet the fenland as a whole has increasing problems of flooding as marine silts pile up against the sea walls and as sea levels rise. The fenland peats are shrinking as a result of better drainage. It is these two stories of seaward expansion and marshland expansion that are the prime concerns of this study. First, however, the scene needs setting.

Terrington St Clement has at its core the 'Cathedral of the Fens'. This large and beautiful church stands above all the nearby buildings and smacks of real wealth. Unlike many villages round the edge of the Fens there are few distinguished buildings nearby. Fenland was wealthy – its churches say so – but its domestic buildings pale into insignificance when compared with those of the south of the county.

Most Norfolk parishes began to take their shape between AD 700 and 1000. The North Fenland place names have mainly *-ton* endings but Terrington and Islington have the early *-ing* component as well. As the section shows, there was an earlier Roman phase in the human history of the north marshland parishes. Later accumulations of silts formed the very slightly undulating surface upon which St Clement evolved. Remaining evidence of

Hay Green: the distribution of Middle Saxon pottery in relation to the roddon system. Map by A. Rogerson and R. J. Silvester, from Norfolk Archaeology XXXIX part 3 (1986), p. 321.

Roman settlement appears only in Terrington St John, where the silt layers have thinned as the effect of marine deposition declines. The major Roman route of the Fens, the Fen Causeway, lay between Burnt Fen, near Peterborough, and Denver; a string of Roman sites lay along that route. The Fens were an important source of corn and salt for the Roman armies. Roman salterns have been found at Elm.[1] Whether the Saxons of the 7th century also made salt is not clear but they certainly settled some of the silt lands and at Hay Green in Terrington a very important mid-Saxon settlement, defined by much Ipswich ware, has been found by painstaking fieldwalking by Rogerson and Silvester.[2] A concentration of nearly one thousand sherds and many animal bones defined a major mid Saxon site which appears to have followed the slightly raised silt ridge of a roddon, or the channel of a former river or creek.

29

Salterns at Terrington St Clement

By about AD 900 the Saxons had begun to develop salt-making again and a major complex of salterns forms an interesting 'hill' area in Terrington between South Green and 'Roman' Bank, the sea wall, covering 120 acres (50 hectares).[3] These mounds represent in part the heaps of burnt ash from the heated salt pans where sea water was boiled off to concentrate the salt.[4] Creeks had to be open to allow salt water to flow in. Sluices had to be built and fuel, presumably peat, provided in large quantities to allow the salt industry to work. Once formed, the salterns also provided slightly higher land for settlement. In 1086 Terrington St Clement had 12 salt pans and West Walton had 24.

E. Miller shows Terrington as one of the manors of the great monastery of Ely and notes that it was the most important of its manors for the provision of salt, providing in 1251 '16 ways' or 672 bushels for the preservation of fish and meat during the winter.[5] Terrington salterns made an important contribution to the economy of this big parish until the 16th century when the Cheshire salt mines replaced sea salt as Britain's major source.[6] Tithes of sheep and wool and also of some cereals would have been sent first in kind and later in cash to Ely. The vicars of Terrington retained other tithes; for example, the glebe terrier in 1716 notes that 'the residue of tithes has lambwool, wood, flax, piggs, geese do belong to the vicaridge . . . to the value of yearly profits of £100 per annum.'[7]

Domesday Book also records the wealth of the marshland parishes in sheep.[8] Terrington could not compete with West Walton's great flocks but in 1086 its two manors had 515 sheep between them; the tenants would have had more sheep as well. Sheep and cattle were to remain important sources of wealth from the eleventh century onwards despite recurring floods and outbreaks of murrain until the draining of the marshland in the late 18th century allowed crops to be grown more widely.

Wills and inventories for the same person exist all too rarely but in 1584 Richard Cooper of Terrington St John left both.[9] He described himself as a husbandman but his inventory was valued at £126 5s 4d. Of this his cattle and horses were worth £35, his sheep £46 and his grain in the loft and crops in the ground £12. It is all to easy to generalise from one example but the emphasis on stock and the growth of wheat, barley, oats and beans as a lesser source of his income is what might be expected from a fen farmer of that period, or indeed earlier or later. In his will his bequests emphasise that his wealth lay in his stock; his wife Ellen was to receive, amongst other things, 20 wethers, 20 'best' ewes and lambs, 20 hogg sheep 'of the best', six dairy cattle and one young mare 'of the best'. After many other bequests of his stock, his servant was to have one ewe and one hog. The servant is to be expected of a yeoman rather than a husbandman. Given the comment made earlier in this section that fenland houses seem to have been of a modest size and quality, this inventory, in contradiction, lists a parlour,

Lovells Hall is the major surviving building of significance in the parish of Terrington St John; it carries a date of 1543 and is perhaps a result of post-Dissolution prosperity in the parish.

a servants' chamber, chamber, hall and kitchen. This snapshot of a late-16th-century fenland farmer gives some idea of the prosperous farming in the extension of Terrington St Clement landward, to form the new parish of Terrington St John.

The impact of the sea on Terrington has already been stressed in discussing the saltmaking industry. There was always the problem of flooding by the sea in the north and by land water in the south. The intricate pattern of fields around the core of the settlement reflects lines of creeks, roddons and man-made banks. As Faden's map shows, a great portion of the parish is north of the Roman bank.[10] This bank seems to date not from Roman times but from the 11th century; Roman remains are several feet under the silts here.[11]

The 'Roman' bank of c. 1100 AD.

The construction of ditches and banks must have been an essential element in the growth of the arable area around the early church on the site of the later St Clement. The pattern of medieval fields on Silvester's map makes this clear. Flooding frequently broke the banks, as in 1316 Terrington and West Walton 'magna pars terrarum submersa est in mare'.[12]

The Civil Wars saw little action in Norfolk but Commonwealth surveys of royal and ecclesiastical manors were made. Terrington St Clement manor was surveyed in 1650 because it was in the hands of Charles Stuart and Henrietta, formerly having been a manor of the bishops of Ely.[13] Surveys such as this provide a priceless picture of mid-17th-century England. The profits of a fair of £3 a year are listed but of particular relevance are the records of the marshes and their value:

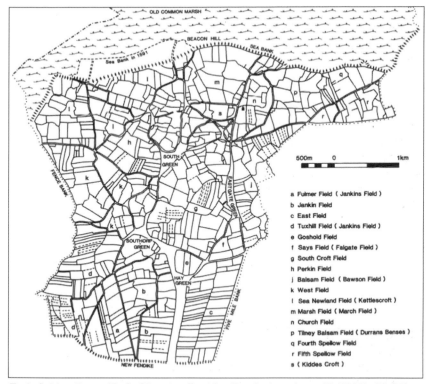

Early field patterns (R. S. Silvester, East Anglian Archaeology 45 (1988), fig. 25).

Marshland called New Marsh now enclosed abuts the sea north and one hundred acres of saltmarsh. 510 acres valued £270 p.a. The occupier being Anthony Williamson Gent.

East Marsh partly arable and partly pasture abutting on the sea towards the north as it lyeth bounded and enclosed with sufficient ditches and banks now in the occupation of Robert Awborne of Clenchwarton 505 acres value £338 6s.

Also listed are

Ewe Marsh and Conyhill Marsh being 24 acres of saltmarsh total 260 acres value £134.

Little Marsh with the sea to the north and the highway from Terrington to West Walton south 14 acres value £8 8s.

33

The charge of maintaining all the sea banks was paid by the tenants during their leases at 1s 11d per acre and this brought in £209 11s 8d. In the same period the Town Book for April 1658 underlines how much the 'town' had to pay to look after the sluices, bridges and banks of the parish.[14] The battle with the sea was a continuous one 'paid to John Osbourne October 3 days for keeping of the Goole [sluice] £1 5s 2d. Paid to William Broadway the 11 of November for hanging the smee gate and for an elme post for the gate to fall backward to 2s 8d.' This was the gate on to the great common grazing of the Smeeth; elm was used because it could stand water well.

The value of the marshes stands out in the survey of 1650 which notes also that the Lord of the Manor had 1,840 acres of copyhold land as well and 'hath the commonage of 200 sheep and 3 great beaste upon the smeeth and fen and droves within the said town . . . with the communage of turbary and reede'. In fact, each tenant had grazing rights for 200 sheep and 24 beasts (cattle, oxen, horses) within the manor.[15] This emphasises the points made from the example of Richard Cooper's will and inventory at least a hundred years earlier. If the area was not flooded and the sheep not diseased it was a grazing region par excellence. The quality of wool was protected and there was concern about fleece colour: the stinting order stressed that 'only white rams should run to every 40 ewes and that there should be no black ram or Ridging kept and go upon the said common.'[16]

Field names such as Sea Newland Field suggest an intake earlier than the building of the main 'Roman' bank. A map of marshland dated 1754[17] quoted by Silvester marks one stretch of the wall as 'gone to sea'. This seems extraordinary as we look at the sequence of expansion shown by Faden marking new walls of 1775 by the late Captain Bentinck and the Common Marsh Bank of 1791, and the draining of Ewe Marsh and East Marsh shown by Bryant in 1826. Later enclosures of the marsh were made by the Crown Commissioners in two stages.

Later sea banks from 1775 to 1970.

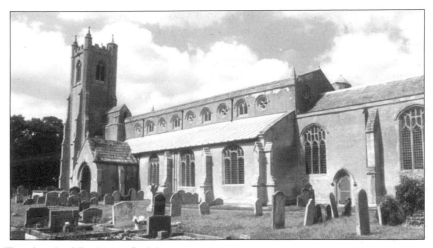

The church of Terrington St John.

The first stage in the expansion of medieval Terrington southwards appears to be the establishment of the New Fendyke which became the boundary of Terrington St Clement. A new community to the south of the dyke on the reclaimed silt lands became Terrington St John. A chapel, later to become its parish church, was established by 1250.[18] The surviving church appears to be of the 14th century with 15th-century additions; the tower may be earlier.[19] A linear settlement grew along the edge of the great droveway which led to Marshland Smeeth and a linear field system evolved as far as the smeeth bank by 1500 as shown in the map on page 27.

In 1796 an Enclosure Act for marshland smeeth and marshland fen was passed. It was 'an Act for draining and improving and for enclosing, dividing

The southern limit of St John's: the Smeeth Bank and dyke.

and allotting certain tracts of common and wastelands called marshland smeeth and marshland fen'.[20] It resulted in the draining of the area from the smeeth drain in Terrington to the old Podyke. In due course this led to the creation of a new civil parish called Marshland St James. After the Act of 1796 a confusing series of small blocks of land was allocated to the several parishes which had previously had grazing rights on the smeeth.

Section XLIV of the Act directed the Commissioners 'to receive claims from the several persons, having or claiming any right or rights of common . . . over the said tract of common shall be required to deliver to the said Commissioners for Inclosure, at their first meeting a specification in writing of the right claim by them . . . distinguishing the freehold, copyhold, leasehold property from each other and within what parish situate and, if copyhold, of what manor or manors such estates are holden'.

We have seen how the Terringtons have evolved seawards in several stages after initial settlement on sandbanks, dykes and later salterns in the area round the church and then landwards into the freshwater marshes to the extent that a new parish of St John was created to the south of the original settlement and the former marshlands have evolved into a new community, that of Marshland St James.

The Brecks: *Weeting*

A regional image of Breckland is perhaps that of twisted Scots pines either side of a stretch of straight road. Another could be that of sheep grazing amongst scattered birch trees and heather with a small mere as a part of the picture (see Introduction). A final one, that perhaps noticed by most as they drive through the area, is that of great stretches of monotonous pine forest consisting of trees of no obvious antiquity. Why so much space and so few signs of settlement?

A breck is an area of land that is, or was, broken up at irregular intervals for cropping. Between these outfields the land, grazed and manured by sheep and rabbits, received sufficient goodness to be cropped again after several years of fallow. The poor quality of the land stems from its thin veneer of acid soils which lie over porous layers of chalk. Archaeological evidence shows that Mesolithic, Neolithic and Bronze Age cultures flourished in this area. Grimes Graves illustrates this very clearly with its scores of Neolithic shafts which were sunk into the chalk to work the layers of flint in it. Neolithic and Bronze Age cultivators cleared the primary oak forest of the area and then, because the soils were so sandy and thin, their fertility was quickly reduced. The sands then turned into heathland and in places began to blow into areas of dune. This sequence can be clearly seen at Wangford Warren which lies just into Suffolk. The two best accounts of the evolution of the Breckland landscape are those by W. G. Clarke[1] and Mark Bailey;[2] there is also a considerable literature just about Grimes Graves.[3]

The parish of Weeting-with-Bromehill has been chosen to illustrate the nature of Breckland. Bromehill was a small settlement around a priory abutting the Little Ouse to the south, Santon to the east and Weeting to the west and north. Weeting, a large parish of over six thousand acres, is bounded by the Little Ouse to the south and the Devil's Dyke to the west and it laps round Bromehill to the east. Grimes Graves lies in the easternmost corner of the joint parish. The pattern of the settlement is that already outlined in the introduction. South West Fen and Fengate speak for themselves; the nucleated village lay near to one of Breckland's few small streams, arable lands lay around the settlement and several thousand acres of heath stretched from the north field to the parish boundary. As the map shows, the pre-enclosure pattern of roads was very different from the later layout. In addition to the prehistoric stages mentioned, the Romans had a landing stage and grain store at Fengate. In the 13th century, perhaps because of the poverty of the land, Sir Henry de la Plaiz founded a priory at Bromehill a short distance from his manor house in Weeting.

The church of Weeting All Saints with St Mary

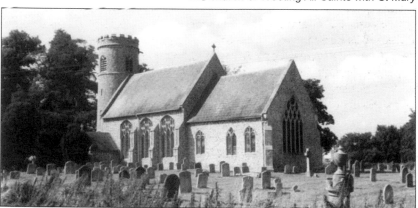

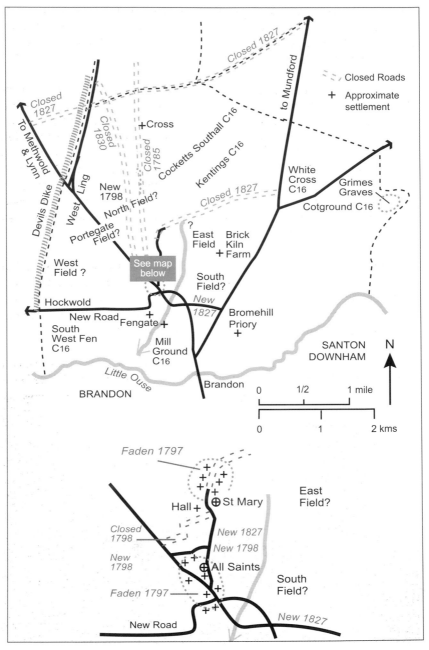

Weeting-with-Bromehill: some medieval elements and later road changes.

A second theme to that of its being a Breckland parish is provided by its 19th-century history when a new estate landscape was superimposed on the 'ancient landscape'. The ancient landscape will be discussed first and then the impact of the Angerstein family afterwards.

Weeting was in fact two parishes, those of St Mary and All Saints, both rectories. The two churches were near one another and the settlement lay around and between them. The earliest map of the village[5] is dated 1760, a survey or dragg exists for 1541/2[6] and a survey of sheepwalks provides some idea of the economy that had survived from Norman times. As the sketch map shows, a former pattern of streets lay between All Saints, the demolished church, and St Mary, which still exists.[7] The dragg of 1541 distinguished several streets, for example, ten plots in Hey Street, and the two rectories were mentioned. The site of the manor was referred to as Castleyards and Faden showed several buildings to the north of the castle in 1797.

Although this is in no way an attempt to outline the history of Weeting, the 'castle' must be mentioned. This was the fortified manor house of the Plaiz family dating from about 1150. The location of St Mary's church may well be related to the existence of the manor. The manor house lay outside the surviving settlement which perhaps flourished under its protection.

The arable fields of Weeting in 1541 were still in late medieval format with an almost classic East Midland layout of East, West and North field. These fields

Weeting 'castle' was actually a fortified manor house.

were subdivided into many furlongs: for example, East field into nine. Brakeney Wong (furlong) in Hangers had many subdivisions and Town Head furlong, in the West field, occupied two pages of subdivisions in the dragg of 1541/2.[8]

Outside the open fields lay a number of individually owned pastures; for example, John Crofts held 100 acres called Kentings 'between Mundford Bounds and the fields of Weeting'. The Lord of the Manor held 200 acres 'between the bounds of Mundford late the monks of Thetford'. There was thus an arc of grazing for sheep flocks to the north of the village. The town (i.e. the villagers) had grazing rights over 400 acres on the south-west fen 'to feed their great cattle and to grave [dig] flaggs [turf and peat].

The survey of sheepwalks that completes the dragg gives details of the flocks and their grazing grounds. It describes, often in a frustrating way, each sheepwalk. For example:

West Linge. the lord hath the said 10 acres, one pasture called West Linge between the ditch and Lynne Way and extendeth from Metholde path on the west of and Well Hill gapp unto the bounds there leading from thence unto Well Hill pit and from thence to Lynne Way to the two crosses containing by estimation nine score acres.

A summary of the sheep flocks at this date lists four, totalling 1,700 sheep, in the lord's hands, three in the hands of Thomas Wright of Kilverstone and a further seven flocks in the tenancy of two farms and the parsonage. This totals 12 flocks and 4,600 sheep. This is a low density over 6,000 acres but it emphasises what the economy of Weeting was based on in the 16th century and for several centuries before that.

The fairly standard Breckland village of late medieval times emerges with meadows and fen by the river, arable land around the settlement and sheep-walks and heaths on the plateau stretching to the bounds of the parish. There was also a warren that covered much of the former parish of Bromehill.

So much then for a fairly typical Breckland parish. Towards the end of the 18th century these nearly empty sandy parishes with their game, rabbits and sheep, could be bought cheaply. Aristocrats, lawyers and merchants began to buy them up and reorganise them. Weeting has gone through at least three phases of change: first came an aristocrat, the Earl of Montrath, from about 1770, he was followed by the Angerstein family; then in World War 2 the impact of the growth of the nearby air bases had its effect on the form of the village.

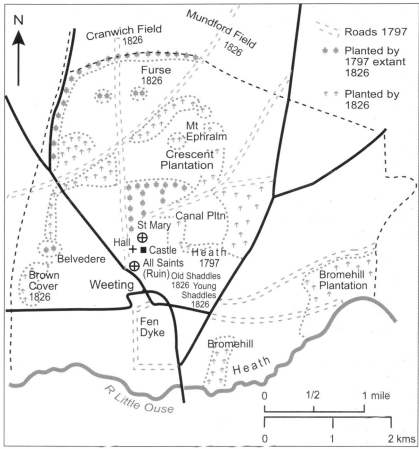

Weeting parish as shown by Faden 1797 and Bryant 1826.

Faden's map of 1797 shows that a number of plantations had already been set out in Weeting. A remarkable collection of bundles of bills has survived that provides a picture of the landscaping activities in which the Earl of Montrath was engaged.[9] In March 1775 he paid £3 13s 6d for 14,700 whitethorn and 10s for osiers. Mention is made of the new road from Wilton to Mundford. In 1776 one Stokes presented bills for £389 16s for work on the lawns, etc; this was a large amount. In 1778 some 87 loads of earth were taken out of the old moat in Hall Yard (i.e. the castle) and a haha was being built by the new hall. The whole nature of the area was being 'civilised'. The tower of All Saints church fell in 1700 and St Mary became the church of the parish. As the maps show, new roads were laid out and old ones closed; this pattern of road closures and diversions is explained more fully in the study of Great Melton.

The Angersteins continued this process after 1805. The story of their acquisition of wealth and then of land is a fascinating illustration of how new wealth, in this case that of a Russian merchant, quickly expressed itself in an old way, that of owning land. They rebuilt the hall and the church and planted 1,000 acres of woodland. Weeting became a closed estate parish, the church became an Angerstein chapel and the coverts their play area.

In 1802 the Earl of Montrath left his estate to Lord Bradford who sold it in August 1805 to the Angersteins. A remarkable inventory of the contents of the house was made in 1802.[10] Only a few items can be selected that give some idea of the contents of a country house of this date – only one of five houses owned by the earl. In the library were 540 volumes and in the Centre Room a further 400 volumes, largely unbound. In the Drawing Room:

> Two pine tables with gilt frames, richly ornamented, and the tops inlaid with inside leather covers to them and green baize outside covers. Three white sattin window curtains lined with white sarsnet and ornamented with silk fringe and tassels and gilt cornices . . . hangings to cover the walls which are hung with white sattin.

The Belvedere had an upper and lower room which had a mahogany wine cistern and two chamber pots among other items. In the stores were 224 bottles of madeira and a further 652 pints of other foreign wines. Home-made wine was stocked in great quantities, for example 152 quarts of white currant wine. In the yards 34 hacking horses were kept, 64 beasts, only a few sheep, including one house lamb and a lamb with a broken leg.

Weeting Hall, from F. V. Luke, A History of the Parish of Weeting *in the Norfolk Record Office [PD 312/27].*

Estate cottages at Weeting.

In the kennel, four pointers, five spaniels and a lurcher. In the barns there was more rye than barley and very little wheat. In 1805, when the estate was sold, it extended to 5,000 acres, including four manors, and its value was estimated at £3,000 per annum. It was described as 'extending over a beautiful sporting country, abounding with game'.

When estate values crashed in the period after 1870 it went through several families until World War 2, when the hall was occupied. The cost of maintaining such houses became excessive after the war and the hall was demolished in 1952. Its site is now covered by recently built housing.

The Broads: *Hickling*

Hickling is famous for its broad, now a National Nature Reserve. Faden's map of 1797 shows the parish to have then had three more broads which are not named but they were Wiggs Broad on the north-east boundary and Gages and Hare Park broads between Eastfield and Stubb field. This underlines the extent to which some broadland parishes have changed their appearance as a result of enclosure and its related drainage activities.

Hickling is a classic broadland parish. It has open water, reed and sedge marshes, alder carr, drainage dykes and former windpumps together with tongues of high quality brick-earth soils between the marshy surrounds. The 'upland' on which the church and part of the village lie is all of 6–26 feet (2–8 metres) above sea level in the west of the parish. The isolated island on which the ruins of Hickling priory lie is about 6 feet (2 metres) above sea level. To the east of Hickling the parishes of Sea Palling, Waxham (once Great and Little) and Horsey lie between it and the sea. Flooding has been a problem for the whole area as from time to time the sea has breached this stretch of coast. A well documented flood of 1607 led to a request from

Above: *Stubbs Mill: an inland drainage wind pump.* Opposite: *Part of Faden's 1797 map.* Opposite, inset: *Reed and sedge on the edge of Hickling Broad, with 'upland' beyond, a haunt of the swallowtail butterfly.*

Ingham Mill

Hickling Priory Ruins

Hickling

Marsh

Wax

Winmere Hall

Hickling

North Hill

Sutton

Mill

John Micklethwaite Esq.

Hickling Street

Hickling Common

Staith House

Pigtech

Hickling Marsh

Crown

Catfield Heath FEN

HICKLING

Cool Harbour Isle

BROAD

White fleet Broad

Catfield

G. Cubitt Esq.
Parsonage

Mill

HEIGHAM

Heigham Holm

South

Potter Heigham

Ludham W. Mill

dham

Ludham Hall

Common

Stream

Coldham

Thurne Fen

Repps

Repps Mill

M

MARSH

Rollesby

L. Mapes Esq.

Mill & Gate
St Benedict at Holm
Abbey

Staith

Thurne

Dam Mill

9

Parsonage

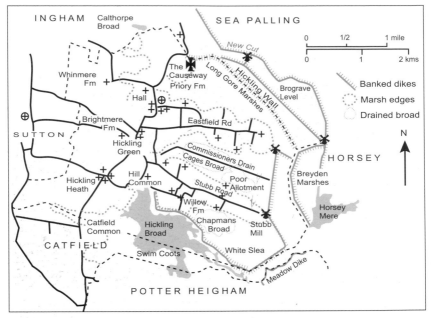

Hickling parish.

those and many other parishes for a Commission to be appointed to whom would be given powers of raising rates to pay for the strengthening of the sea defences.[1] Faden, on his map of 1797, and Bryant, 1826, both show sea breaches on this stretch of coast.

The village lies in three parts: a nucleus around the church and market place; a rather sinuous settlement on what was Hickling Green; and a small cluster at Hickling Heath, which reaches the Staithe. A market charter was granted in 1204 and a fair in 1227.[2] Scattered, isolated farmhouses lie in the former East field and Stubb field. Faden marks several buildings on the northern edge of Stubb field which were probably marshmen's cottages, of which Brackenbury Farm may be the only survivor. There is only one major house, Hickling Hall, dated to 1700, of seven bays and built of brick.

Hickling had, again typically of the Broads, a dual economy based on agriculture and marsh. A yeoman farmer, Robert Cocke, who made his will in 1646,[3] was a man of some importance and in his will he was able to leave four small estates, one to his wife and three, almost certainly, to his three daughters and their husbands. He had bought two of these estates, presumably with the intention of providing inheritances for his family. His lands

Typical Hickling buildings. The older buildings (there appear to be few before 1700) are cottages rather than houses – that is, they are single storey with dormers in the thatch. This contrasts with Ludham where there is a number of handsome 17th- and 18th-century houses sited at the head of Womack Water. Hickling Staithe does not seem to have led to the same degree of growth.

Hickling staithe.

were both freehold and copyhold and he termed them closes, crofts and marshes. The examples imply that enclosure was already well advanced and he made reference to lands that 'do now lye enclosed'. He left his grandchild a close of 14 acres and his bequests of at least two marshes make it clear that not all marshland was in common ownership by 1646. Amongst field references were East field, West field and Stubb Close. He still located land by reference to former medieval fields.

Hickling was bounded to the north, east and south by marshes or water. Domesday Book (1086) gives us no clue as to wastes or their uses but the cutting of peat from wet valley floors provided a main source of fuel for broadland until about 1500. As is now well known, the broads are drowned peat pits; the cutting of peat increased greatly from about AD 1200 until about AD 1350 as the population increased. More was cut than was needed locally and the peat cuttings provided a surplus for sale and for use in abbeys and nearby towns. Hickling Broad, created by the flooding of 1287, has an average depth of 6 feet (2 metres). It is unlikely that it was ever drained after that flooding and peat working could only have continued by dredging with scoops. As well as the 1609 flood others also brought sea water into the Broad. For example, in 1792 the freshwater fish in it were killed by salt water. Large amounts of peat were also used for salt making and Domesday Book recorded 122 salt pans in East Norfolk.[4] None were actually related to Hickling but Edric of Laxfield had half a salthouse in Sutton.

The importance of Parliamentary enclosure acts is stressed in several parishes in this study. That for Hickling in 1801 affected 1,527 acres, changing the layout of the parish by draining three small broads. A new straight 'Commissioners' Drain' was cut between East field and Stubb field. It is probably no accident that Hickling Green (Street) was sited at the head of the former arm of marsh. New mills were built at East field and Stubbs mill, to take the water from the new cuts and pump it into Meadow Dyke. The drained marshes were allotted to claimants whose claims were based on their upland ownership, ownership of qualifying tenements and common rights. They dug new dykes and a rectangular pattern of individual holdings was created. Often these were still used in a traditional way: cut for turf, hay, litter, sedge and reed.[5] Common rights were acknowledged by the allocation of some land for the use of the poor, either directly or by letting it and using the income to help the poor by buying coal, for example. Hickling's poor allotment was laid out over the drained area of Hare Park Broad.

William Smith, better known as 'Strata' Smith, a father of modern geology, wrote in a letter to Heigham enclosure commissioners, about 1804–7, saying that if 'they agreed to the draining of Hickling Broad which I have long and most sanguinely wished to accomplish a great part of Heigham Sound may also be laid dry . . . and the watery waste to become a useful property'.[6]

Hickling Broad.

This landscape, often flooded by sea breaches of the dunes to the east, had common grazings for sheep, cattle and wild mares and produced a wide range of marshland products and wildlife; now it was tamed. Through the foresight and benevolence of Lord Desborough and others, Hickling Broad and its neighbouring marshes were protected from the improvements in agriculture that affected the rest of the parish between 1800 and 1870.

Hickling Priory: remains of the chapter house.

Hickling Priory, a small house of Augustinian canons founded in 1185, used a tiny island site in the marshes to the north of the parish church.[7] Like Thorney, or even on a larger scale Ely, the isolation of an island site had its attractions. What we now see is but a tiny remnant of the Augustinian site. At the dissolution Hickling, like Ingham, fell into the hands of the Wodehouse family of Waxham Hall. This pattern of wealthy families becoming even wealthier by such acquisitions is one that will be met again. As so often happens, a legal dispute of 1601 (in this case within the Calthorpe family) resulted in an interesting document in which a description of the priory site was given.[8]

> All those houses standing upon the site of the Priory of Hickling,
> the mansion house
> brewhouse with the millhouse adjoining
> the long stone granary
> the long stone house at the gate
> the dairy house
> old dove house
> all the houses, edifices and buildings upon the site of the said priory

standing together with the orchards, gardens and pond yard with a certain close called the Horse Close being whole site of said priory environed or encompassed with ways and old ditches – 50 acres 3 roods.

Nearness of the sea, an easily breached coast, fen marshes and gentle upland with rich soils set the scene for Hickling. Man's early peat cutting activities creating broads, the arrival of the railway to bring holiday-makers and the foresight of early conservationists held a balance between the natural environment and the tourists that it attracts and have been the elements that make Hickling what it is today.

River valleys: *Brampton and Burgh-next-Aylsham*

The River Bure rises near Melton Constable on the back slope of the Cromer Ridge, a great glacial end moraine. As a result of the melting of the ice large amounts of melt water flowed south off the ridge carving the valleys of the Ant, Bure and Wensum. The modern River Bure meanders across a wide flood plain and this provides the meadowland for each of the riverside parishes. The pairing of parishes along the river valleys has already been mentioned and Brampton and Burgh-next-Aylsham straddle the valley of the Bure downstream of Aylsham. This is a beautiful stretch of Norfolk valley landscape where the meandering river twists across a wide, often marshy, valley floor between low river bluffs. Cattle-rich meadows survive between the arable slopes on either side of the

Burgh church on a terrace above the flood plain of the Bure.

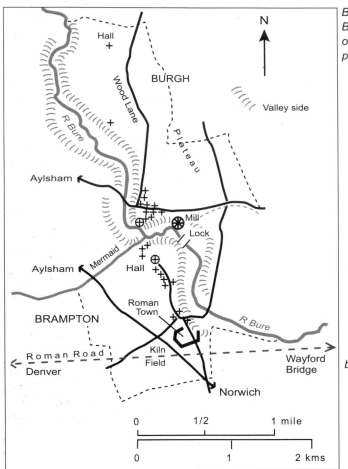

Brampton and Burgh: layout of the two parishes.

Opposite: *Plan of archaeological survey of Brampton in 1973–4. The heavy line shows the position of a defensive ditch, the small circles within it some excavated kilns and the rectangular blocks the sites of buildings. Map by C. Green from East Anglian Archaeology 5 (1977), fig. 12.*

valley. That is as far as the mirror image goes. Once we start to look at the evolution of the two villages, two different stories emerge. Brampton conceals the site of an important Roman town and pottery making centre. Burgh has no such evidence but it has a magnificent Early English church as well as a watermill and a canal lock.

Sir Thomas Browne wrote in 1667 of the urns found at Brampton.[1] This is the first known reference to one of Norfolk's Roman sites. The brick-earth, forming the surface of the plateau into which the shallow river valley was cut, provided a perfect material for the Roman potters. It is almost pebble free and it provided the clay for Norfolk's beautiful orange-red bricks from

1500 onwards. The Romans found this deposit, perhaps after laying out their important road from Denver to Caister by Yarmouth. Brampton lay just to the north of this road and a Roman 'Stoke-on-Trent' developed, supplying pottery and tiles to a wide area.

In 1966 the Brampton study group was set up and directed by Dr A. K. Knowles; by 1977 it had identified 141 pottery kilns to the west of the town. Iron working had been identified in the area as well.

A defended Roman town lay at a junction of two Roman roads, one of which ran from Water Newton (Durobrivae) across the Fens to Denver via Billingford to Brampton and on to Caister by Yarmouth or, perhaps, a Roman fort which has since been eroded by the sea. The other ran from

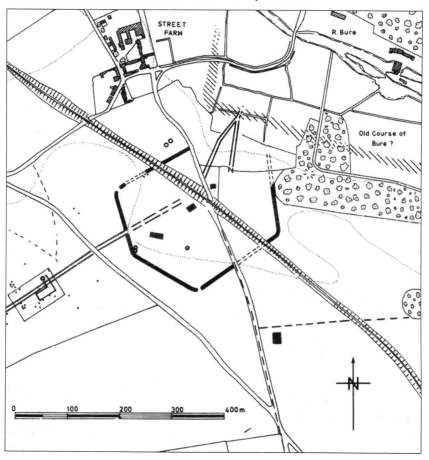

Caistor by Norwich (Venta Icenorum) through Stratton Strawless, Brampton and then, more debatably, on to the north coast. In 1973–4 Christopher Green directed an excavation to the west of the Roman town.[2] The map shows that a road running south-west from the Roman town cuts through a swarm of pottery kilns. This may have been a service road to the kiln field or, more likely, a road running south-west towards Attleborough.[3] Green's report notes at least 140 kilns from which came Roman mortaria and flagons at the peak of the industry in the second century. He comments:

> At that period the stamped mortaria from Brampton were finding their way to the military markets of the north, raising Brampton to the status of not only the most important local production centre but the leading Icenian export industry, competing with those at Colchester, the Verulamium region and the Mancetter-Hartshill field.[4]

Later, timber buildings were erected in the excavated area and pottery production continued into the fourth century. Brampton's importance in Roman Britain was an early example of the way in which many Norfolk villages have been linked to much wider national and European patterns of activity.

When the Romans left Norfolk about AD 410 they must have left a small industrial town. Did the Saxons who settled the area in the 5th and 6th centuries name it

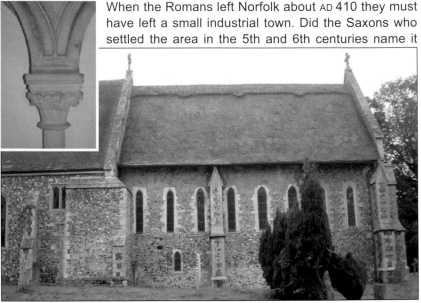

Burgh church: exterior of the chancel, with inset *detail of chancel arcade.*

Above: *Burgh mill survives as an interesting cluster of buildings grouped around the river channels.* Below: *The lock below Burgh mill is still there, but no longer functioning. The great flood of July 1912 destroyed all the locks on this navigation as well as those on the North Walsham and Dilham Canal, ending the attempts to improve the Bure and the Ant.*

Brampton because of the evidence of burnt earth and pottery lying about or because of the broom growing on the derelict spoil heaps and over the kilns?[5] Brampton and Burgh are both Saxon place names. No evidence has been found in either of their parish churches of any Saxon work. Did Christianity exist at Brampton in Roman times? Did it survive into later periods? We do not know. Brampton has a round tower considered by Pevsner and Wilson to be of the 12th century. The church stands high above the River Bure at the north end of the village street. The Roman site lies at its southern end and to the south-west of the present settlement.

Across the river on the terrace of the Bure lies Burgh church. Viewed from the south, the length of its Early English chancel is striking; inside it is stunning. A long chancel, lower than the nave, has beautiful gothic arcading stretching to the east wall. Above the arcade are eight lancet windows on the south side and a three-light east window. Pevsner and Wilson date it to between 1220 and 1230; this was a period when Burgh was a royal manor, and it may be that royal beneficence contributed to the chancel. The excellent church guide reminds us never to believe all that we see. The eastern two bays of the chancel, the east gable and window and the reredos are all the results of carefully correct restoration in 1876–78 by R. M. Phipson, 'with suggestions from Scott'.[6] The additions are difficult to see inside the church because Phipson so carefully copied the earlier work.

The River Bure was navigable from Yarmouth as far as Coltishall and in 1779 the Bure navigation was established by a number of East Norfolk gentlemen including a Walpole and a Marsham. Like all transport projects, the building of the canal took longer and cost more than was originally planned. It opened Aylsham and the villages between it and Coltishall to trade by wherry and led to the growth of Millgate in Aylsham. The wherries could carry 18 tons and drew three and a half feet (a metre or so) of water. There was no towpath.[7] The parish boundaries which followed the river course were crossed by the new cuts for the navigation, as at Burgh mill. The lock below Burgh mill is still there, but no longer functioning. The great flood of July 1912 destroyed all the locks on this navigation as well as those on the North Walsham and Dilham Canal, ending the attempts to improve the Bure and the Ant.

It is typical of almost every riverside parish above the highest tidal points that a watermill exists, or existed. From Domesday times, watermills were a perquisite of the lord of the manor; in Burgh, Roger Bigod, the Earl, held half a mill and unusually a free woman, Maerwynn, held Burgh and she held one mill.

The Bure valley has twinned parishes along its course from Itteringham to Acle. The river meadows and marshes widen downstream and become more significant; they were cut for peat below Wroxham; Acle had an important cattle market for stock brought off the marshes in winter. The physical environment played a major part in the development of the settlements. The brick-earths were not used everywhere but the Romans made use of them at Potter Heigham, as well as Brampton, and at Ludham from the 1600s brick kilns produced the attractive orange Norfolk brick that could be shipped away by water. Peat cuttings filled with water and reed and sedge beds became major elements in the landscape below Wroxham.

River valleys: *Bawburgh*

Bawburgh is an example of the valley-side parishes discussed in the introduction. It is unusual in that it is a cross-valley parish stretching from watershed to watershed across the valley of the Yare some five miles upstream of Norwich so that it has the basic format of two valley-side parishes. A church settlement lies to the south of the river and a riverside cluster to the north. The floor of the Yare valley is wide and flat and consists of rich meadow land. In 1987 it was clear why the valley floor had not been settled when a lake formed for some distance either side of the mill. The basic physical layout has a complex historical overlay from the Bronze Age onwards. It brings the historian into the realms of legend, that of St Walstan, and raises the problem of where history ends and legend and

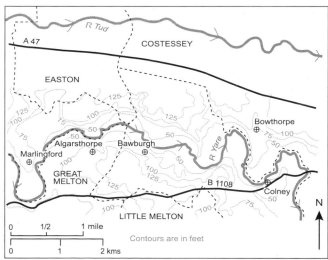

Bawburgh bridge.

folklore begin. It also has several interesting buildings, in particular two enigmatic ashlar buildings, a watermill site and a demolished hall for which documentary evidence survives.

Tumuli survive as evidence of Bronze Age activity and the *Historical Atlas of Norfolk* shows evidence of Mesolithic, Neolithic and Iron Age finds in the area. This is all linked to the layout of river terraces and supplies of flint from these, or from the chalk, into which the Yare cuts as it drops to sea level through Norwich. The impact of Roman settlement from about AD 65 to 400 may be a factor in the shape of the parish. The Roman road from Caistor St Edmund to the Fen Causeway ran to the south of Bawburgh and there is evidence of several set-

Late Bronze Age tumuli on Bawburgh Heath, drawn in 1957 by Harry de Caux. Drawings given to the author by Harry's sister Alice de Caux.

Bawburgh mill and its millstone today.

tlements, a hoard and perhaps a Roman road running, unusually for such roads, along the valley floor.[1] This reminds us, as over so much of Norfolk, just how heavily settled and farmed Norfolk was in Roman times.

The name 'Bawburgh' is an interesting one. In Domesday Book it is spelt 'Bauenburc'. The *burgh* element often implies a fortified site, or in East Anglia a barrow site; it can also mean a hill. That Bawburgh was an outlier of the Domesday manor of Costessey suggests that 'barrow' rather than 'fortified site' may be the explanation, especially in view of the two drawings by Harry de Caux.

Domesday Book also noted that Bawburgh had a mill and the surviving watermill is a classic example of continuity and change. The site is almost certainly that on which the Domesday mill was built. Once a break of slope is established mill pools banked and overflow channels cut, the site of a mill becomes fixed. Like so many of Norfolk's watermills this has changed its role in its later history. It was no doubt an important manorial asset to the manor of Costessey. In the 19th century, once steam-powered milling developed, it lost its importance and like so many mills it had to be rebuilt, as happened in 1887. Kelly's Directory of 1908 notes that it was a watermill, occupied by D. Child, a baker, so it was still producing flour. In 2005 the mill remains a key point of attraction but it has been converted into desirable residences.

Domesday Book makes no reference to a church in Bawburgh in 1086, yet the legend of St Walstan tells of his funeral in the church in 1016 which was conducted by Bishop Aelfgar of Elmham. St Walstan, to whom the church is dedicated, jointly with St Mary, was an East Anglian saint. It was as a saint of agriculture and agricultural labourers that he was venerated, though whether this was immediately after his death or some time later is not clear. A side chapel or shrine was built on the north side of Bawburgh church. This was demolished after the dissolution and only the footings can still be seen.

The history of St Walstan has recently been fully covered in a very well researched study by Carol Twinch.[2] She quotes M. R. James as writing of St Walstan as 'obscure . . . a mythical personage' and Eamon Duffy noting 'that the cult of St Walstan as being contained within a 17 mile radius of Bawburgh, thereby highlighting the local emphasis'.[3] Images of St Walstan survive on church screens at Barnham Broom, Denton, Litcham, Beeston-next-Mileham, Ludham, North Burlingham and Sparham.   He is usually shown with a scythe, sceptre and two calves.

Briefly, the legend is that Walstan was a holy man, probably from Bawburgh but also held  in great regard in Taverham and Costessey at the

'Hermit's House' and 'Slipper House' (former summer-house), with detail of the former.

time of his funeral. In 1016 Aelfgar, Bishop of Elmham, allowed his remains to be venerated as those of a saint. In 1047 Bishop Aethelmar of Elmham dedicated the church to Saints Mary and Walstan and a shrine chapel to St Walstan. Walstan's simple life of kindness became a model to all though there is no evidence that he was actually canonised by a pope. His dying prayer was for the workers and brute animals, and for his final return to Bawburgh he relied on two bulls yoked to his cart.[4]

A spring to the north of the church, according to the legend, burst forth when the cattle stopped there on Walstan's last journey. It was later capped and the resulting well was deemed to have healing powers; Twinch notes that these were still respected in the early 19th century and that several pilgrimages to the church were held, the last in 1989.

The chapel on the north side of Bawburgh church was presumably built in 1047. How this was served is not clear but in 1240 William de Ralegh, the Bishop of Norwich, appropriated the rectory of Bawburgh to the cathedral priory. This meant that the great tithes of Bawburgh went to the priory and that it would benefit from income from the shrine. The priory allocated the income from Bawburgh to the office of the sacrist. The sacrist supervised the fabric of the cathedral, its furniture, vestments and all expenses relating to the services.[5] The income did not go all one way: in 1320 the repair of the chancel of the church, a rectorial responsibility, was undertaken by the sacrist. Here, as in so many Norfolk churches especially in the Fleggs, we have an example of the important link between the priory and many villages throughout the county. This link continued still in 1739 when Say produced his detailed map of lands held by the Dean and Chapter, the post-dissolution successor to the priory in Bawburgh.

Church Farm, Bawburgh, originally built in 1278.

The shrine to St Walstan drew pilgrims to it and in 1278 a building to house priests and pilgrims was built to the north of the church. This survives as Church Farm. A team of six priests served the shrine. Buildings along the road from the bridge to the church would almost certainly have earned a few pence in putting up pilgrims. At its peak the shrine would have carried statues and candles and would probably have been brightly painted. The sick came hoping for cures at the well.

In 1538 the shrine chapel, like that of shrines everywhere, was destroyed when the priory was dissolved. A formerly busy, religiously important village lost its major raison d'être and returned to being the agricultural community which Walstan's life had symbolised.

Ashlar blocks reused in a later building.

What happened to the shrine? When we look carefully at several of the buildings on the north side of the bridge they can be seen to have cut limestone blocks in them. These blocks were shaped for other structures and the so-called 'Hermit's House' and 'Slipper House' (illustrated on p. 60) have many more in them. Was the shrine built from this expensive ashlar? The Ordnance Survey maps note the site of a 'hermitage' by the bridge. There has been much discussion about this but Twinch concludes that it was unlikely that there was a hermitage there.

A survey of the lands held by the Dean and Chapter after the dissolution gives a good picture of how 73 acres were distributed in 1488.[6] Say's map of 1739 suggests that little land had been lost by that date for it maps 35 separate pieces. Many of the 'strips' shown on the map are of the standard furlong in length, for example numbers 19 and 24 in the great field. By 1739 it is only because of the care of the Dean and Chapter in keeping records that strips are shown that by then were in closes (for example, pieces 25, 26 and 27 in the croft). Whether they were farmed separately by then, or as the land of Mr Norris, is an open question. The perambulation way shown on the map is the parish boundary along which the parishioners would walk once a year in order to make

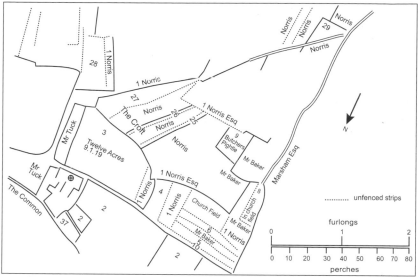

The lands of the Dean and Chapter in 1739. Simplified from a map of 1739 by I. Say in the Norfolk Record Office [Church Commissioners Map 11894].

it quite clear which lands were in Bawburgh. A wood called Malliswonge of 10 acres was listed in 1488 and is probably the same as the smaller wood shown on the 1739 map. The timber was a valuable asset for building repairs, fuel and perhaps for acorns for pigs in the autumn. The survey gives a nice description of the site of the rectory of Bawburgh in 1488:

The church of St Mary and St Walstan, Bawburgh, from the south-east.

> The sacrist of Norwich holds the rectory of Bawburgh which lies between the messuage of Richard Marchant formerly lands of the cathedral church on the east and the tenement Erbald on the west and abuts on the great road of the king to the church of Bawburgh to the south and on the common on Bawburgh called Lokholme to the north.

In 1601 the will of Thomas Harvey,[8] a Bawburgh yeoman, was proved and an inventory of his moveable goods was also made.[9] We learn that he held land from Carbrooke manor and Costessey manor, reminding us of the complexity of the manorial system in Norfolk. He left lands '3 akers in 3 peeces' in the church field as well as other pieces and some meadow to his elder son, John. His younger son was to have various lands and '5 neate cattall and all my houses' on condition that he looked after his daughter Margaret. Two daughters each got a bullock and one a milch cow. He left his servant five shillings.

His inventory recorded six milch cows, two heifers and a calf, two geldings, one mare, three foals, five pigs and one sow. There was wheat, meslin, rye, barley, hay and vetches in the barn. The house was of two storeys with chambers over the kitchen, dairy and parlour. The ground floor had kitchen, hall, parlour and dairy house with eight bacon flitches. His inventory totalled £33 2s 4d. This is the lower end of the yeoman spectrum; it gives a picture of a small farm with scattered landholdings, but its owner was able to leave all his children land or animals and give 3s 4d to the repair of the church and 3s 4d to the poor of the village.

Bawburgh in 2005 retains its individuality as two attractive riverside settlements linked by a bridge, a church and a mill. The former shrine of St Walstan stands high on the south bank of the river at the western limit of the settlement. It is still a farming community but the mass production of ducks has replaced traditional farming. Smart executive houses have been woven into the site of the Hall using a lot of limestone ashlar. The north and south boundaries of the parish are busy roads leading to the new fringes of Norwich, the hospital and the university and Bowthorpe respectively. The line of the Norwich southern bypass now defines Norwich and provides the eastern boundary of Bawburgh, dividing a rapidly growing Norwich from what is still a rural parish.

River valleys: *The Shoteshams*

The East Anglian landscape, unlike that of the Yorkshire Dales or the Welsh valleys, generally lacks clearly defined physical units apart from former islands such as Wormegay or the Fleggs within which groups could settle. However, some small valleys do exist as well as the larger valleys of the Bure, Wensum, Yare and Waveney. The River Tas drains central south Norfolk northwards to join the Yare, and the hundred of Depwade very broadly corresponds to the area of the upper drainage basin of that river. Shotesham Beck, a tributary to the east bank of the Tas, drains a small basin which is a natural unit that defines the present Shoteshams, formerly the

The valley of the Shoteshams, showing the relative positions of Hall, park and parish churches.

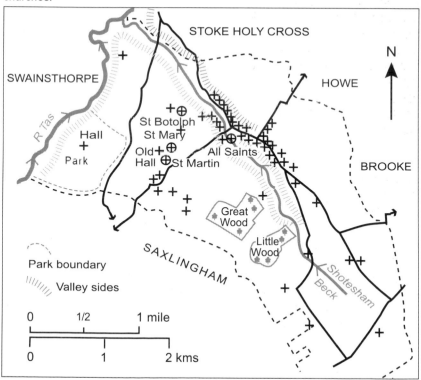

parishes of Low and High Shotesham but before that the four parishes of All Saints, St Mary, St Martin and St Botolph.

The Shoteshams lay in the hundred of Henstead. It was one of the smaller of Norfolk's 33 hundreds. The Domesday Survey of 1086 used the hundreds as the administrative units within which vills were recorded. They therefore existed by 1066. This is not the place to discuss their origins but they remained the units of administration within the county until the Poor Law Unions were created in 1834. They were the units through which taxes were collected and national returns of all sorts were reported.

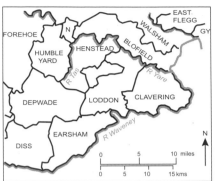

Left: *The hundreds of south-east Norfolk.*

Below: *Henstead hundred with its constituent parishes.*

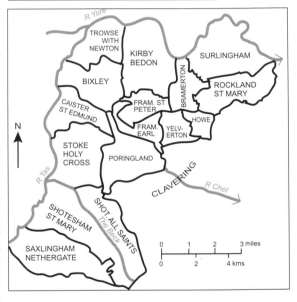

Some hundreds were held by particular lords; for example, Mitford was held by the Abbot of Ely. Parish constables collected taxes and submitted them to the constables of the hundreds who returned them to the sheriff. The shapes of hundreds vary but the rivers Tas and Yare form the western and northern boundaries of Henstead hundred.

In looking at the origins of a settlement the archaeological record is vital and the place-name may also be helpful before the first documentary evidence becomes available. For most Norfolk settlements the first written evidence is to be found in Domesday Book, 1086.[1] Norfolk Landscape Archaeology maintains a Heritage Environmental Record (HER) for each parish. The record for the Shoteshams runs to 167 pages and records finds from the Early Palaeolithic through to the standing buildings that have been listed by the government as of historical interest. Some key points from the Shotesham HER are brought out in the following sections.

The Shoteshams lie only four miles south of Venta Icenorum (Caistor St Edmund). The main Roman road from Colchester via Scole, the Pye Road, followed the west side of the Tas Valley and it is probable that a second road followed the eastern boundary of the Shoteshams. The valley sides of the Beck provided well-drained areas for two big Roman sites in the upper valley as well as some lower down. At least two important sites, however, lay on the boundary with Saxlingham on the plateau. Until about AD 400 the area was part of a Romanised landscape. However, Caistor and Long Stratton (the *ton* on the street, i.e. Roman road) are the only two place-name clues to reflect the Roman occupation.

The really interesting question is to what extent any Roman sites survived and in what way Saxon settlement began to take place. Did woodland recapture areas formerly farmed by the Romans? No large collection of mid-Saxon pottery (Ipswich ware) comparable to that of Hay Green in Terrington (page 29) is recorded, but the work of metal detectorists, encouraged by Norfolk Landscape Archaeology to bring in their finds for identification, reveals a thin scatter of Saxon metalwork and some later Saxon Thetford ware in the western half of the parish.

The Shotesham valley: downstream (looking north-west) from All Saints Church.

All Saints' church, Shotesham, standing high above the Beck.

The general impression over Norfolk is that early Saxon settlement (AD 500–750) was relatively sparse compared with mid and later Saxon settlement.[2] Saxon burial cemeteries form one of the most distinctive elements of early Saxon settlement. No such cemetery exists in the Shoteshams; two have been found near Caistor St Edmund and three at the head of the valley of the River Chet. Metal detectorists have however found a variety of metal objects such as brooches and pins in the Shoteshams.

The *-ham* ending to the place-name is now accepted as implying an early Saxon origin, about AD 500 to 600. The *Shote(s)* element can be read as being in the genitive and various place-name texts suggest it is derived from 'scot' or from 'shott'.[3] Does this imply a person or a group of Scots settled the area? However, the word for a slope, *scyter*, offers a more likely explanation for the siting of what is now Shotesham All Saints.[4] The development of four separate parishes with the same overall name suggests a 'pupping' of the original 'ham' as ownership sub-division, by gift or inheritance, took place or new settlements were created in the considerable area of the waste of Shotesham.

It would therefore seem to be a Saxon influence that gave the name to Shotesham. Where would the first settlers have chosen to live, and why? The site of All Saints Church dominating the valley of the beck seems the obvious location for an early settlement with water, meadow and drained

St Martin's church remains on the plateau.

hillside. The other three churches are within very short distances of one another on the wet clay plateau amid what may well have been woodland (the last remnants being Little and Great Wood), and perhaps were the result of later settlement. Why three separate parishes should evolve so close to one another is more difficult to explain.

A charter in the St Benet at Holme cartulary of the time of King Edward (1043–66), regarded by West as specious, makes reference to the church

Well drained valley side fields: All Saints tower to the north.

of St Martin and lands which belonged to Brictrith.[5] This argues for a pre-conquest date of St Martin. A 12th-century charter makes reference to payments of corn to be rendered to the hall of Shotesham, implying that St Benet's had a manorial site.[6] Smith quotes Bryant as referring to St Botolph being given by Canute (1016–35) to St Benet's.[7] These references support the idea of the two parishes of St Martin and St Botolph existing on the plateau before the Conquest.

Shotesham has one of the most complex and confusing sets of entries in Domesday Book for Norfolk. They are summarised below. The difficulty is to relate particular entries to particular settlements and to individual churches. The Domesday entries refer to Roger Bigot, the Earl of Norfolk, having half a church (was this All Saints?) and the Abbey of Bury St Edmunds one quarter of a church (was this St Mary?). It seems that two churches are implied in Domesday Book as existing by 1066, the other parts perhaps being accounted for as being built by the communities rather than the lord. Morris argues, however, that this was not a frequent event.[8] The Domesday entry for the part of Shotesham held by the king distinguishes the 'other Shotesham'; this implies two settlements but with no mention of a church. If we look for architectural evidence, no Saxon work has been found in any of the four Shotesham churches. St Mary at Howe nearby is firmly recognised as of Anglo-Saxon date and it also incorporates Roman tile.[9] Pevsner and Wilson note that the former church at Framingham Pigot had a Saxon tower.[10] Were there earlier wooden churches in the Shotesham area? Was Howe a minster church from which daughter churches developed?

The Domesday total of heads of households in the Shoteshams is 118 which, with a multiplier of 4.5, gives a population of 531. As well as clusters of villagers, smallholders and slaves in the two main entries for those of Roger Bigot and St Benet at Holme, there are several entries relating to freemen. Williamson discusses the distribution of freemen in his *Origins of Norfolk*.[11] He suggests that they represent families much less tied to the manorial system, having rights to their land and perhaps reflecting movements into parts of the vill which were still empty. However, he suggests they do not correlate with areas of woodland where perhaps they might be 'assarting' their new holdings. It is clear that St Martin's and its surrounding settlement formed the early manor held by St Benet's.

In 1332 a tax known as a lay subsidy was levied at a rate of one fifteenth on the value of goods surplus to those regarded as necessities. for the Shoteshams 125 names were listed, which if multiplied by 4.5 gives a total of 562 people. Those paying less than 8*d* were exempt so that the actual figure will have been rather higher.[12] Population rose steadily during the 14th century and the Shoteshams may perhaps have reached 700 people by 1349.

In 1348–49 the Black Death struck England. It is recognised that perhaps one third to one half of the population died, but it is more difficult to find the exact extent to which a single place was affected. Bishop Bateman was Bishop of Norwich 1344–55 and his register, covering the period of the Black Death, gives a picture of the extent to which the clergy of the diocese were reduced.[13]

The register records that John London, chaplain, was instituted to the Vicarage of St Mary and St Botolph on 13th August 1349. The Bishop nominated him; Pentney Priory held the rectory (the two churches had been consolidated in 1322). On the same day John Matlask, priest, was instituted to the rectory of All Saints of which Pentney also had the patronage. On 18th August Adam de Westwyk, priest, was instituted to the rectory of St Martin; Edward III was patron because St Benet's does not seem to have had surviving clergy. It is unlikely that all four parishes would normally have lost their clergy at the same time but the Black Death was still at its peak and the Shoteshams were badly affected. It is probable that the lay population also suffered severely.

Shotesham St Mary church lies next to the Old Hall. Around the Old Hall is a complex pattern of earthworks with toft platforms and a hollow way. These

St Mary's church, Shotesham.

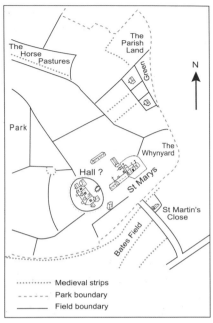

Part of Shotesham c.1650, from a map in the Norfolk Record Office [FEL 1077]

are sufficient to suggest that, at some date, a settlement existed that was related to the Hall, a manorial site, and to the church of St Mary. St Martin's church also lay near to the Old Hall, while St Botolph's church lay just to the east.[14] The simplest solution is that the earthworks belonged to the parish of St Mary and that other settlements lay south and east of St Martin and north and east of St Botolph. However, given the example of Great and Little Wacton glebe and tithe patterns, it may be that these three parishes were inter-mixed. An agreement in 1187 between Sir Robert de Vause and St Benet's suggest that some rationalisation of ownership between St Mary and St Martin did take place.[15]

In 1517 an enquiry into enclosure noted that rights of tenants to pasture on arable after harvest had been withdrawn and that one area had been enclosed by the lord.[16] Smith concludes that desertion finally came about in the fifteenth and sixteenth centuries 'owing to oppression by the lord of the manor'.[17] The Black Death (1349) may well have been an initial factor in reducing the population of the St Mary's area. The map of 1650, showing part of Sir William D'Oyley's estate, marks a few buildings between the Hall and St Mary's Church and two isolated cottages. It confirms that the 'village' of St Mary had largely gone by 1650.

In 1536 the possessions of St Benet's Abbey were transferred to the Bishopric of Norwich and these included St Martin's Church. In 1538 the possessions of Pentney Priory were sold to Thomas, Earl of Rutland, and these included the advowsons of All Saints and St Botolph. By 1588 Christopher Greenwood held the livings of All Saints, St Mary and St Botolph.[18] All Saints had 100 communicants in 1603 and St Martin had 60 communicants but it was in ruins in 1746.[19] By the early 18th century the parishes were merged so that the Shoteshams had returned, in religious terms, to the one unit from which they probably began.

In looking at the surviving two churches, All Saints and St Mary's, we must be careful. Smith points out that St Mary's was in a ruinous state in the 17th century and that it was not until 1879 that R. Fellowes, the rector of Shotesham, put it into a usable state. By about 1700 it would seem that only All Saints was functioning, reflecting the decline of the population around the hall.

The plateau: *Wacton*

Depwade hundred

The hundred of Depwade was one of the 33 medieval hundreds of Norfolk. (A hundred was an administrative unit and it has been suggested that it may have been an area which could provide one hundred fighting men or held one hundred hides (12,000 acres) of land.) It consisted of 20 parishes

Depwade hundred.

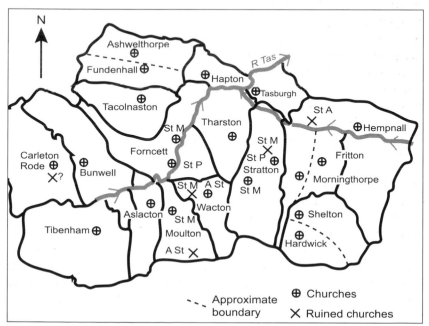

73

and was, typically of South Norfolk, one of the smaller Norfolk hundreds. This begs the question of how early the administrative organisation of Norfolk, or of other English counties, began. The name of a hundred often designated the meeting point for the men of the hundred and it would be expected to have been central. The vill of Forncett stands out as the key vill of the hundred and perhaps the Depwade (deepwade?) was a crossing point of the never very deep River Tas.

Depwade lay only a few miles to the south of Venta Icenorum and the Roman road from Colchester to Caistor (as Venta Icenorum has become) cut through the centre of the hundred, Stratton (the *ton* on the *street*) being sited on it. It is not surprising, therefore, that Roman finds have been made along the line of the road and also in Wacton on the south-facing slope of the small valley. To what extent this part of Norfolk carries any influence of an Iron Age landscape is a much discussed question.[1]

The post-Roman period of this area may have been one of woodland recovery on the wet clay plateau. Field-walking has shown little evidence of Saxon settlement. In place-name evidence only Tibenham suggests an early Saxon name; the 'tons', including Wacton, are Saxon secondary place-names.[2] The -*wick* of Hardwick and -*thorpe* of Morningthorpe suggest later, perhaps Danish, settlements. Forncett became the major settlement

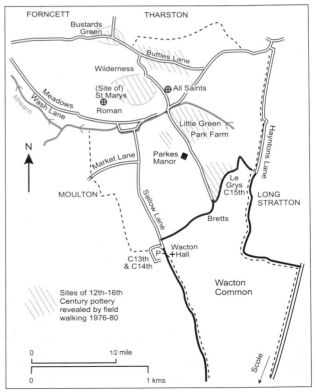

Wacton parish, showing early settlement sites.

of the hundred before 1066 when it was given to Stigand (Archbishop of Canterbury 1052–70). He was given the central part of the hundred. He was deposed in 1070 and his holdings went to Roger Bigot, Constable of Norwich Castle and Bailiff of all the King's holdings in Norfolk after 1077. He held 187 manors in Norfolk and was one of William I and William II's great servants.[3] Forncett thus continued in descent to the Dukes of Norfolk who held it and many outlying pieces of land, for example in Wacton, in the 16th century.

Wacton is a parish typical of the wood pasture zone of central and south Norfolk. This is the account of what were two parishes in Depwade Hundred, those of Wacton Magna and Wacton Parva, which now form the parish of Wacton. It can be viewed as a parish that occupies part of the Tas Valley system and also as a parish of the south Norfolk boulder clay plateau. A small east bank tributary of the River Tas drains the northern part of the parish and the south-facing slope of this shallow valley provided a site for Roman and medieval settlement. The heavy clay on the plateau must have been difficult to plough until improved methods of field drainage began to be used. It must have remained as wet, heavy land, perhaps as surviving woodland. Two Wood Greens in Long Stratton were probably former woods and perhaps Wacton Great Common may have survived as woodland until late medieval times. Sylvia Addington showed that several hedges in the area contained many species and may be the surviving edges of ancient

The Great Common, Wacton.

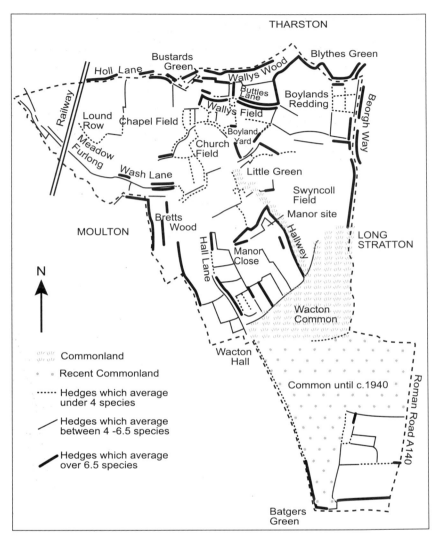

Map (after S. Addington, Norfolk Research Committee Bulletin *24 (1980)) showing ancient hedges in Wacton parish.*

woodland.[4] In north Wacton three areas of woodland, Wally's Wood, Hobbawood and Brett's Wood, all survived into the early 16th century.

Field work between 1977 and 1981 by members of the Norfolk Research Committee, now a part of Norfolk Archaeological and Historical Research Group, resulted in the discovery of large quantities of medieval and post-

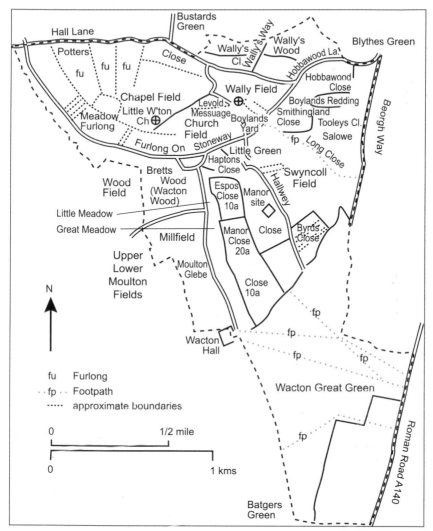

Wacton in the sixteenth century (after C. Barringer, B. Cornford and A. Davison, Norfolk Research Committee Bulletin 18 (1977)).

medieval pottery on sites not now built on. Several buildings were also studied including the White Cottage (a 14th-century hall), le Grys Farm (perhap 16th-century) and Grange Farm (early 17th-century), which are amongst a number of timber-framed buildings in the parish. Buildings such as these show that Wacton must have been a community of prosperous yeomen between about 1400 and 1600.

Above: *Le Grys Farm, a 16th-century timber-framed screens passage farmhouse.* .
Below: *The White Cottage, a 14th-century timber-framed open hall.*

The two churches reflect very different developments within the modern parish. All Saints, the surviving round-towered, early-14th-century single-cell building with Decorated windows, sedilia and doorway, suggests that there was wealth in the parish in the

All Saints, Great Wacton (now Wacton): early wealth.

1300s. St Mary's, on the other hand, was already regarded only as a chapel by 1565. In 1254 it was regarded as 'pauper nihil'.[5] A survey of 1602[6] recorded:

> Wacton Parva, alias St Mary. The sayd church ys decayed about three or four score years since [1520], the steeple whereof ys at this present converted to a dovehouse by John Lavyle of Wacton.

According to White's Directory the two rectories were merged in 1522 so these two dates tie up quite closely. Was this the result of a partial decay of the settlement or simply the result of the merging of two manors? The latter would seem to be the more likely case.

The main area of medieval settlement stretched from Wilderness Farm and St Mary's Church down the slope to All Saints Church and then around the Little Green. There was also a scatter of settlement along the north edge of the Great Common. A wide strip of common linked the Green to the Great Common which until 1939 occupied the southern third of the parish. The Great Common and the Little Green covered 269 and four acres, respectively, when surveyed in 1533.[7] Why should such a common have survived and why is there still of common of 82 acres today? There was no parliamentary enclosure award for Wacton and this explains survival until 1940. The manor of Forncett was the chief manor of Depwade and there is a long and complicated entry in Domesday Book. It was a Bigod manor and in the 16th century all management of the common lay with Forncett, a manor of the Dukes of Norfolk, and not with the Manor of Parkes of Wacton. Given the grazings for cattle on the marshes of the Waveney Valley flood plain

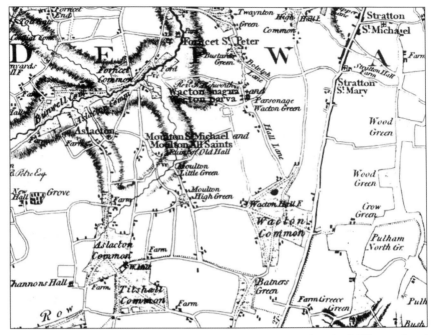

Faden's map of 1797 shows many commons in Depwade hundred; Wacton Great Common was the largest.

meadows the Great Common may well have been a valuable staging post on the way to Norwich Market.

It was also important for the stock of the tenants because there were 162 rights of common held by them and 18 rights by the poor. A right was defined in the Churchwardens' Accounts of 1699–1715 as the right to graze two neat beasts or four sheep.[8] There were six bull runs: horses were permitted after 25th July, after neat beasts were taken off; two horses were equal to three neat beasts. The Wacton Overseers' accounts of 1673 to 1683 have entries for expenses on the common such as the provision of gates.[9]

During the 19th century holdings were gradually amalgamated but no attempt was made to enclose the common. In 1940 the Ministry of Agriculture compulsorily purchased it. In 1955 the Agricultural Land Commission acquired the southern 190 acres despite a great fight led by Dr Joyce Mellor, whose records relating to the common have survived in Norfolk Record Office. Compensation was paid for the loss of 163 grazing rights. In 1959 the remaining 20½ common rights were bought by three people so that they controlled the grazing of the surviving 82 acres. At least the surviving 82 acres are now registered so that a part of the Great Common and all the Little Green remain to remind us of what was once a major grazing area in South Norfolk.

Wacton is fortunate in that an unusual tithe survey taken in 1541 has survived. It is an invaluable document in many ways, produced in order to clarify which lands in Wacton paid tithe to All Saints Church and which to St Mary (the chapel). In doing so it describes each piece of land, names the tenant, gives the manor to which it belongs, gives its acreage and the names of the furlong, the field or the close within which it lies as well as the names of the many roads and lanes. It is mainly from this survey that the 16th-century map of Wacton (page 77) was constructed.[10]

A brief transcribed extract from the survey is given, starting with the 20th piece in the chapel field:[11]

20th   In the tenure of William Lavyll holden Tyth to church & chapel
2 acres   of Richemond. free   Molton Mychell evenly
                                                                    devyded.

21st   In the tenure of Richard Botyld parcell   Tythe to church
1 acre   of Hemnalls. free   Botyld sayeth

22nd   In the tenure of Richard Botyle holden of   Tythe to chapel
1/2 acre   Molton Hall. bond   Botyld sayeth

23rd   In the tenure of William Lavyll holden of   Tythe to chapel
1/2 acre   Aslacton. free   Botyld sayeth

24th. la.   The glebe land of the chapell

25th   In the tenure of Thomas Reve holden of   A dowbt of tithe
la. lr.   in the manor of Forncett of the tenement *Kettles*
               More Howsse

26th   In the tenure of John Seman holden of [?]   a dowbt of tithe
1/2 acre   Mr Dewke. bond *Marcon*

27th 1[?]   The glebe land of Seynt Peter of Forncett Tythe to chapel
                Forncet glebe   Botyld sayeth

Even this short extract underlines the complexity of the manorial structure of this part of Norfolk, five manors being mentioned. The extract covers part of Chapel Field in Wacton yet the manors of Forncett, Aslacton and Moulton hold land there. Glebes too were scattered with a piece of Forncett glebe in the field. Despite this careful survey there was still doubt in two cases about which church tithe was payable to. The tenants of each piece were named so that a list of tenant farmers in the parish in 1541 can be constructed.

Wacton Hall, as surveyed by Alan Carter (drawings held by Geoffrey Kelly).

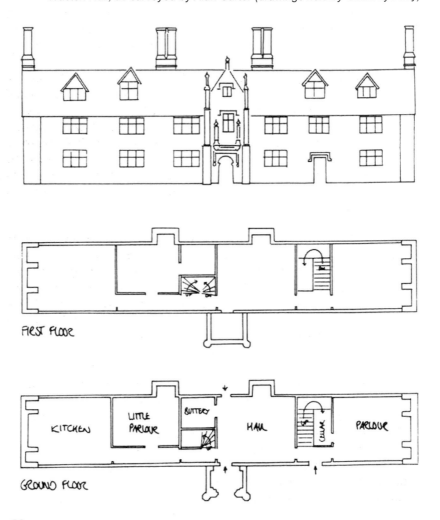

FIRST FLOOR

GROUND FLOOR

KITCHEN

LITTLE PARLOUR

BUTTERY

HALL

CELLAR

PARLOUR

The term 'tenement' was applied to one holding. The tenement More Howss lay within the manor of Forncett. A tenement included a house or cottage and perhaps 15 to 30 acres of arable and grazing land that made up the holding. Frequently these holdings carried the name of a tenant of some time ago and became 'fossilised'. As time went on, bits and pieces of land were exchanged, so that by 1541 a tenant farmer might hold pieces that were originally parts of several ancient tenements and in describing them it was convenient to use the old tenemental name.

This survey and other manorial records make it possible to name open fields, closes, woods and road names with reasonable accuracy. The picture gained is one of the decline of the open field system with several named closes in a formerly well-wooded parish (see the map on page 77).

So much for landscape. Who were the tenants mentioned in the survey, and what sort of lives were they leading? Several fine timber-framed houses have survived in Wacton; why should this be? It was a wood-pasture village on wet clayland, so timber was the best locally available building material. The doyen of local/landscape historians, W. G. Hoskins, drew attention to the 'great rebuild' of 1560–1640. As he comments, 'by the 1570's to 1670's the wealthier yeomen had begun to build themselves larger and better houses. Sometimes they added to or reconstructed their ancestral dwelling'.[12]

It is rarely that wills and surviving buildings can be tied together. In an excellent study of Wacton Hall Geoffrey Kelly managed to do this.[13] John Sherman of Wacton (died 1597) was a 'gentilman', according to his will. He was able to leave his wife Barbara £40 a year, he left each of his two daughters £200. His son Timothy, when he inherited, was to provide the annuity for his mother and the sums for his sisters out of the income for his lands. John's bequests of goods for his wife give a vivid picture of the contents of part of a prosperous household.

> Item I gyve and bequeth vunto my saide wife the bed whereon she nowe lieth fully furnyshed as it now standeth in her owne Chamber and the best bed furnyshed as it now standeth in the newe parlor chamber and also thoccupacion of the presse there standinge and after her decease I will that the same presse shalbe and remayne vnto Tymothie my sonne his executors or assignes and to be and stande where it now standeth Item I gyve vnto my saide wife all suche Chestes as her owne lynnen and apparell lieth in now beinge in her

owne Chamber with all suche thinges as in them doe nowe remayne and alsoe one spitt one brasse pott one kettell one skillett pan one rostinge yron one payre of Andyrons with three Rackes three platters three dishes Three sawcers Three porrengers one trencher salt of sylver and guilte one goblett of sylver one tinne of silver one pott of silver which was Mr Drakes her fathers and thre spones of silver Six Cushinges of Tapestry and thuse of one longe table in the newe parlor with two covered stoles and one Chaier of waynescott

Significantly, he left his wife:

my new parlour and newe hall with the chambers over the same with the garden adioyning to the same and the little yarde called the Chickens yarde and house with the chamber over the same.[14]

The late Alan Carter, former director of the Norwich Survey, carried out a detailed survey of Wacton Hall. His plan shows how his analysis of the building linked up with Sherman's will and helped to show how the building developed. The analysis shows how a 'traditional' three-bay East Anglian farmhouse gradually progressed up-market in the 17th and 18th centuries and the original central chimney stack was removed when the parlour was added.[15]

In 1592 an inventory of the goods of George Raynes of Wacton was taken.[16] John Sherman of Wacton Hall was one of the appraisors and George's goods were valued at £78 8s 3d. Like all inventories it provides a mass of detail about one who must have been of yeoman status. Only three blocks of the information are quoted.

In the chamber over the buttery	£	s	d
2 boards and one square piece of timber	0	0	6
4 sacks	0	2	0
one woolen wheele	0	0	12
one pair of stock cards	0	0	12
one pair of woll cards	0	0	06
two stone of hemp	0	6	00
three stamping beetles	0	0	02

In the cheese house

4 ferkins plus 2 kilderkins for?

2 fleting dishes	0	0 02
1 cheese press	0	3 00
eyght chese breds and ?	0	5 00
12 boules	0	5 00
one great boule	0	2 00
one churne		

The cattell

4 ould keyes plus 4 heyfers	12	0 00
3 old mares and 2 more colts		
8 plus 20 sheep old and young	11	0 00
one sow three shotts		
3 geese		
12 hennes one cock		

The corn

5 combes plus 2 bushells wheat
8 bushells peas
6 combes one and a half bushells barley   [no values given]
10 combes plus one bushell otes
8 bushells of meslyn
3 combes of fetches

It is always dangerous to generalise from one document; however, given that the wood-pasture nature of South Norfolk is generally accepted, the cattle, cheese house, spinning wheel and wool cards add a pastoral flavour to the fairly standard mixture of grains in store. Perhaps this reveals a picture of mixed farming rather than one heavily focussed on stock, with extra earnings coming from spinning hemp and wool and from cheesemaking.

These selections from a will, an inventory and a building plan, can only give a flavour of the economy and lifestyle in Wacton in the 16th century. There were many poorer people than the two examples given; some of the smaller houses have almost certainly decayed and disappeared. It is the homes of people such as John Sherman and George Raynes that have survived or even have been added to.

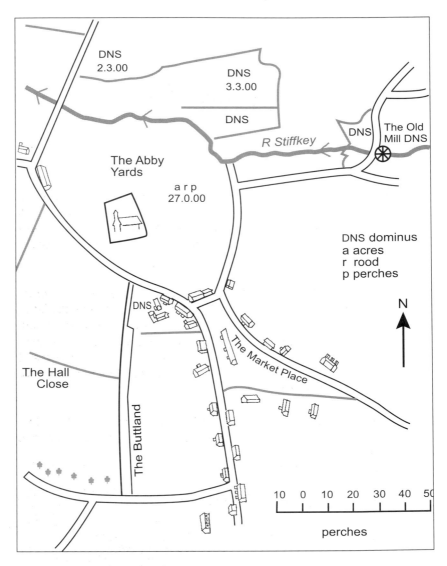

Binham about the year 1655, based on John Brooke's redrawn plan of 1733 in the Norfolk Record Office [Hayes Storr 10]. A perch was a unit of linear measure equal to 16½ feet (5 metres) and also a measure of area equal to 30¼ square yards (25.3 square metres; there were 40 perches to the rood and 4 roods to the acre). The priory precinct crosses the small stream which provided it with water for the kitchens and its lavatories.

The Impact of Man

A Benedictine priory: *Binham*

The ruins of the Benedictine priory and its surviving nave dominate the skyline north of the village of Binham. By a series of happy accidents the priory precinct, together with the gateway, have also survived so that, like Wymondham, the impact of the medieval building and its dominance of the settlement is all the more striking.

Binham, Langham, Field Dalling and Saxlingham occupy the valley of an east bank tributary of the River Stiffkey. This small tributary forms the focus of these villages rather than being a boundary. A second small stream meets it upstream of Binham village and the main part of the settlement lies on the south side of that valley. The undulating sands and gravels of the Cromer ridge provide dry soils through which the shallow valley floor provides a tongue of grazing land.

Present-day Binham is a small village which was formerly, like Cawston, a market town. It is concentrated around a triangular market place and fairstead where three small roads *Cottages between the main street and the market place.*

meet and lying to the south of the precinct of the former Benedictine priory. Outside the gatehouse of the priory, cottages line the road to Wells as far as Westgate Farm.

Prosperous 17th-century houses at the south end of the market place.

Buildings within the village provide an attractive mixture of cottages and one or two more imposing buildings. Careful examination shows that, in the predominantly flint fabric, bits and pieces from the priory have been used. The attempt to provide modern vernacular houses using traditional shapes but sea-rolled flints rather than field flints used for centuries in the other buildings is questionable.

The modern vernacular: new building on the market place.

88

The photograph opposite shows the steep gable of a large house and the Flemish gable of another: perhaps early- and late-17th-century buildings, respectively. These probably replace timber and plaster buildings, for in 1625 the Court Book records

> It is found by the homage that Robert Page has allowed his tenement copyhold of this manor to be in decay on account of defects in the roof and plaster work. Therefore he is in mercy 3d. And he is ordered to carry out sufficient repairs before the feast of St Michael Archangel next upon pain of 3s 4d.[1]

This chapter is concerned primarily with examining the impact of the Benedictine priory on the development of the settlement. Binham already existed as a Saxon settlement with a watermill and a manor hall. This is an unusual Domesday Book reference; even less usual is the record that there were eight horses at the hall in 1066, reduced to five by 1086. The modest settlement of 18 families had a further 16 freemen, perhaps Danes, reflecting the nearness to the coast.[2] Peter de Valoines, nephew of William I, received 17 lordships in Norfolk, one of which was Binham; his base was at Orford Castle in Suffolk.[3]

It seems that Peter and his wife, Albreda, had founded this cell of the Benedictine Abbey of St Albans by 1093 but the foundation charter dates from 1104. The priory was laid out on the traditional Benedictine plan with the great church (of which the nave survives) and the cloister and monastic

Binham Priory: looking from the chapter house to the ruined choir.

buildings to the south. Its outstanding surviving architectural feature is its west front, as Pevsner and Wilson say:

> If what we see is really of or before 1244, i.e. before Westminster Abbey, it is the first example of its style in the whole of England and amazingly up to date even from the French point of view.[4]

The architectural gradation in the nave from pure Norman (Romanesque) through to the Early English (Gothic) at the west end is a fascinating example of a major stylistic change in English architecture. Sadly, the central tower and the choir have gone.

Binham Priory: the Early English west front, c.1240.

To the south of the church the cloister survives in plan, as do most of the associated buildings, which are typical of those of a major Benedictine house. The use of field flint for walls and of Caen and Barnack stone for quoins is clear. The west front, in its lower courses, is fully faced in imported stone.

The impact of the priory on Binham and its area spread far wider than that of the surviving precinct. The alignment of the former road from Stiffkey and Cockthorpe and that from Wells and Warham was adjusted to run round the boundary of the precinct. The de Valoines endowed it with an income with the tithes from Dersingham and Ingoldisthorpe and the tithes of the manors of Ryburgh, Snoring Tofts, Testerton, Little Ryburgh, Wood Dalling, Saxlingham, Walsingham, Barney, Babingley, Appleton and Pattesly. King Henry I (1100–35) granted a Wednesday market, a fair of four days and

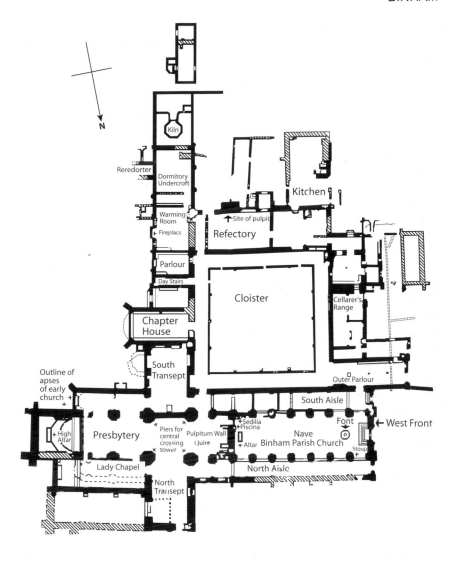

Plan of Binham priory, after D. Install, Binham Priory: a Guide to the Parish Church of St Mary and the Holy Cross *(Binham Parish Church Council, 1991).*

free warren on all their lands. In addition to these tithes all sorts of additional pieces of land were acquired by gift and at the dissolution the *Valor Ecclesiasticus* valued it at £140 5s 4d. This compares with Castle Acre, valued at £306 11s 5d, and Bromholm at £100 5s 3d. The *Victoria County History* states that 21 Norfolk villages made payments of some sort to Binham.[5]

In return for some of this income Binham would have helped the sick and poor in its area and it probably would have had a school in which the brightest young boys would receive an education in Latin and music; some of them might have progressed to an Oxford or Cambridge college.

Binham was not only a religious centre for a wide area but an economic one too. The founding of a fair and market would have given a living to many traders and craftsmen such as butchers, fish merchants and stonemasons who served the needs of the monks and their lay population.

By the 17th century the houses around the market place were being built of flint and brick and a number had chimney stacks, as can be seen on the map extract on page 86. They are shown as cottages, not as two-storey houses. Only three houses are shown as having three stacks and puzzlingly none is on the site of the handsome building at the south end of the market place. Remnants of the little row in the middle of the market place may have survived until now. It is another puzzle why none of the buildings in Westgate shown in a map of 1792 was on the map of 1655.[6] Such an attractive map as that of 1655, redrawn in 1733, would seem from its overall detail to be reliable but these

Remains of the market cross in Binham.

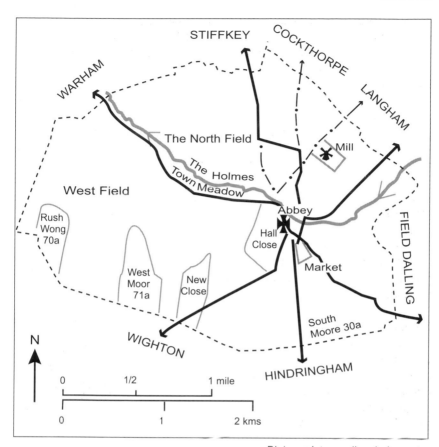

Binharn: late medieval elements.

questions remind us that all sources must be used with care.

The diagrammatic map of Binham above is based on the large 1655 map and on many references in Birstall's transcripts.[7] The stream divides the parish so that the valuable meadowland lay down its centre from the Abbey precinct to the Warham boundary. A north field and a west field occupied large areas. The map of 1792 shows that traces of the open field system still remained in those areas.[8] They were finally extinguished in the enclosure award of 1814. There are several mentions of saffron fields in the Birstall transcripts. Saffron was grown for its yellow dye which was used in the cloth trade.

Sheep were certainly a part of the 17th-century economy of Binham. In 1625 Robert Hall was found to 'have overburdened the commons of

Binham called South Moor and East Moor by feeding on them more sheep than by reason of his tenure he ought to have done. Therefore he is in mercy of 3*d* and is ordered not to do so any more upon pain of 10*s*'. This was a general pattern of dealing with manorial transgressions; a small fine was charged initially as a warning and if no improvement resulted the larger fine would be charged at a stipulated future date.

By 1626 there were, at least in Binham, controls upon public behaviour being imposed and it was found that the same Robert Hall, the sub constable, 'has played at cards and other forbidden games and has also permitted forbidden games in his house at Binham contrary to the provisions of the statute (33 Henry VIII Cap. 9)'.

Birstall has made a painstaking transcript of the Binham enclosure papers which is very clearly written.[9] Unusually, the Act of 1814 was promoted by four small landowners. There was still debate as to the line of the parish boundary with Hindringham over the south common. The Lord of the Manor, Thomas Clarke, held 1,700 acres, which gave him a major controlling interest in the parish. The role of the commons and of common rights is well illustrated by Sarah Mase's claim submitted at the beginning of the process of enclosure. She held six and a half acres of enclosed arable land, one and a half acres of meadow and a messuage copyhold of the Manor of Binham. She claimed:

> Right of common pasture for all her commonable cattle levant and couchant thereon upon and over all the commons and waste grounds in Binham (except the common called the New Close) at all times of the year. And also to a right of common or shackage for all her great and commonable cattle levant and couchant upon the aforesaid lands and premises in, over and upon all the commonable fields, half year or shacklands in Binham and the New Close according to the usage and customary mode of exercising rights of common and shackage thereon.

She also claimed rights of cutting whins, furze and rushes upon the said common and waste grounds for necessary fuel. The rights of shack, that of putting stock on to harvested fields, was a valuable one to the tenants and it also meant that their stock manured the land. The award had therefore to take this loss to the tenants into account in determining the amount of land allotted to them from the common. Sarah Mase was compensated for this in the award.

Binham lost its priory in 1538, it lost its commons bit by bit and they were finally enclosed in 1814. By that date its market and fairstead no longer functioned. The practice that Henry VIII adopted of selling off monastic sites meant that the Paston family gathered up another property and that the major holding still existed as a unit in Mr Thomas Clarke's hands in 1812. Binham survives with one of Norfolk's outstanding monastic remains, an exceptionally fine parish church and a small cluster of attractive flint and brick buildings around its once busy market place.

Wool, Cambridge and Woodforde: *The Mattishalls*

The Mattishalls (Mattishall and Mattishall Burgh) lie very near the centre of Norfolk on the boulder clay plateau between the Rivers Yare and Wensum. The shallow valley of the little River Tud forms the northern boundary to the parishes (now a single civil parish). These parishes have no particular characteristics in their physical layout that can be seen to have any influence other than this near-centre position. As will be shown this position has been of great significance.

The Mattishalls in their setting.

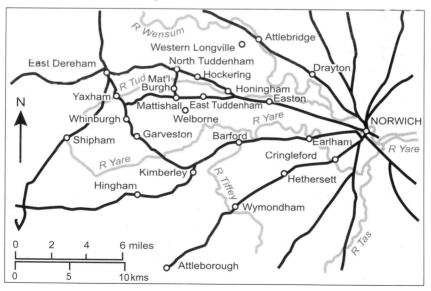

Two churches dominate the plateau landscape. The larger, All Saints, stands out well amongst a group of attractive houses around Church Plain, the focal point of the parish. St Peter's, much smaller, lies on the edge of a small group of houses, several of which are early buildings of some quality.

What is now a fast-growing commuter village was, until about 1950, two distinct settlements, neither of which had castle, large manor house or monastic remains to distinguish it from scores of other Norfolk villages. The themes that have gradually come to the fore in the history of the two parishes are those of the late medieval wool trade, Parson Woodforde and Gonville and Caius College, Cambridge. All three themes show how places are intimately linked to networks of other nearby, more distant and overseas worlds even though they lie on an apparently timeless site of a few square kilometres of central Norfolk.

Chronologically the link with Gonville Hall, Cambridge (as it then was) comes first. In 1370 Edmund Gonville, a Norfolk man, endowed his new foundation of Gonville Hall with the rectorial income of Mattishall All Saints. This meant that the income from the great tithes which were paid by parishioners to the church was to go to help the costs of the new college. In return Gonville Hall had to maintain a vicar to look after the church. He was to have

All Saints church with Robert Foster's Lady Chapel.

the small tithes and the income from the glebe land to maintain him. If the chancel of All Saints was to need repair then Gonville Hall had to provide the necessary finance. Mattishall All Saints, like so many Norfolk Churches, had in this way a link to an outside world of Cambridge and favoured Mattishall boys would have access to Gonville Hall, later to become Gonville and Caius College, to study there.

St Peter's church, Mattishall Burgh.

This Cambridge link was further strengthened when Elizabeth I's Archbishop Matthew Parker, a Norwich man, married Margaret Harleston, the daughter of Mattishall man Robert Harleston, in 1547; she died in 1570 and the Archbishop in 1575. Margaret left some land in Mattishall to the parish,

Margaret Harleston's house.

part of the income of which was to pay for a Fellow of Corpus Christi College, the Archbishop's college, to preach the Parker Sermon at Rogationtide, a custom which still survives.

The records of Gonville and Caius list Mattishall scholars after 1370. Many of these would have gone into the church, the law and later, after Dr Caius added to the college in 1557, into medicine. Others might, under the Parker link, have gone to Corpus. So an apparently rather isolated Norfolk community had links with Cambridge colleges and through them with the Inns of Court in London. In 1585 Richard Baldwin's son Henry, aged 15, went up as a pensioner to Caius College. He was educated in Mattishall and Colchester. Does this imply a link with the Colchester textile world? Then Thomas Baldwin went up to Caius in 1590 as a pensioner. He probably became rector of Mattishall Burgh. His will was proved in Norwich in 1620.[1]

The second theme that shows how the Mattishalls were linked to the outside world is an even more important one, summed up in one word – wool. This is when Mattishall's situation in an almost central position in the county seems to have been of great importance. The map shows some features of the distribution of fold courses and sheep flocks. Evidence from selected estates shows the large number of flocks kept by families such as the Le Stranges, Fermors and Heydons. Norwich Priory wool as well as that from Mattishall is known to have gone to Suffolk.[2] In 1529/30 Thetford Priory accounts record 6d paid to entertain a woolman at the Angel.[3] He presumably bargained to take the priory clip, or some of it. A network stretched from flock to woolmen, to spinners to weavers, to major merchants such as those in Norwich and clothiers such as the Springs in Lavenham. This network linked villages and market towns together and employed large numbers of women and children as well as weavers. In this way, a second layer of wealth to that gained from corn, sheep and cattle added to the prosperity of the area.

A series of references in the Norwich Mayor's Court Book make it clear that a group of prosperous wool dealers (broggers) was based in Mattishall and that they were avoiding the Norwich wool market and its concomitant taxes and selling wool direct to the other markets, especially into Suffolk for the Suffolk broadcloth trade as

Wool broggers on the Mattishall village sign.

exemplified by the Spring family of Lavenham. Hudson and Tingey[4] give the following details from the Mayor's court held on Saturday 30th May 1562:

Court on Saturday, 30th May [1562]

Woll Chapmen – Robert Tylney of Matsall Bergh hath sold cc stone to men of Suffolk. John Howlett of Hockering sellyth no woll but only in Norwiche Markett or at home among his naybors. Richarde Baldewyn of Mattashall hathe solde ccc stone woll to men of Suffolk. Alice Peeres of Matshall Bargh sellyth no woll but only in Norwich Markett. Thomas Wattes, the elder, Thomas Cressolde, Edwarde Wattes, Roger Wattes, John Wattes, Thomas Wattes the younger, William Partryke [and] Nicolas Allen. All thes persons do by woll and bring none to Norwich Markett but lode yt and sell yt to the Clothers in Suffolk.

Keith Allison listed 33 'middlemen' from Mattishall and Mattishall Burgh in his appendix to his dissertation on the Norfolk textile industry.[5] This pattern of activity may reflect the cussedness of Mattishall men but is also interesting in that it shows how the whole cloth manufacturing industry of East

Selected flock and foldcourse distribution 1500–1600 and wool movement.

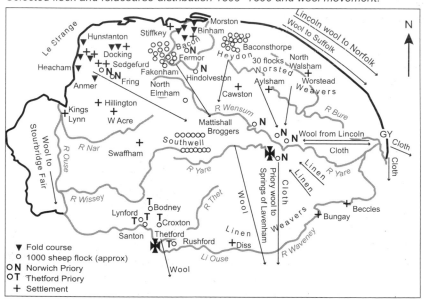

Anglia was interlocked. The shorter-fibre Norfolk wools were better for the coarser cloths. Whether Mattishall was a gathering point for the long-fibre wool for the famous worsted cloth is not clear. A number of fine 16th-century houses survive in the Mattishalls.

Most of the 'broggers' listed by the Mayor's court extract and in Allison's longer list were extant in the later 16th century and many very interesting wills survive to illustrate their wealth. Richard Baldwyn's is a good example; he died in 1587, leaving four sons and five daughters.

- To Richard he left his Mattishall lands.
- To Henry his lands in Terrington St John.
- To Robert his lands in West Walton.
- To Thomas his lands in Welborne and Brandon Parva.
- Mary received a silver spoon and £20 out of Terrington.
- Charity received a silver spoon and £20 out of Terrington.
- Francis a bed from the hall, a silver spoon and £30.
- Margaret received a silver spoon and £20.
- Judith received a silver spoon and £20 from the Mattishall land.

Richard's ability to leave lands to four sons reflects his wealth. That Henry had land in Terrington and Robert in West Walton suggests that the Baldwyn sons had provision of a wool supply to their merchant father very well organised. It is interesting to speculate whether Henry and Robert

A brogger's house.

reared Lincoln long-wool sheep on the Fens for the worsted production.

One 'woolman' was Robert Foster and as he died in 1507 his will was of the pre-Reformation type and it is possible to see from it how at least parts of Mattishall All Saints Church benefited from wool wealth and how the Lady Chapel was added to the existing 14th-century building. The following extract shows how much he gave to the existing fittings of the church as well as his major gift to the fabric and gifts to several neighbouring churches. (Were these parishes from which he bought wool?)

> And my body to be buried in the
> Chapill of Ou[r] Lady in Matsale to the which high altar
> in recompens of my tithes forgotyn I bequeth 6s 8d. Item
> to Seynt Nicholas light 2d. It[e]m to the white torchis 2d. Item
> to the repuren[?] of the church of Matsall 6s 8d. Item to
> the Popular light 12d. It[e]m to our Lady Light in the reed loft 4d.
> It[e]m to the basin 4d. It[e]m to yche of the gilde lights w[ith]ynne
> Matsale 20d. . . .
>
> It[e]m I biqueth to Welborn Church 3s 4d. It[e]m to Hokerying church
> 3s 4d.
> It[e]m to the church of northtuddenh[a]m 3s 4d. It[e]m to the church
> of Borough 3s 4d. It[e]m to the church of Esttudenh[a]m 6s 8d.
> It[em] to thrixston church 3s 4d . . . It[e]m I bequeth to the
> makyng of a Chapell of Our Lady in the est ende of the
> Suthale in the church of Matsale £10 4s on the which

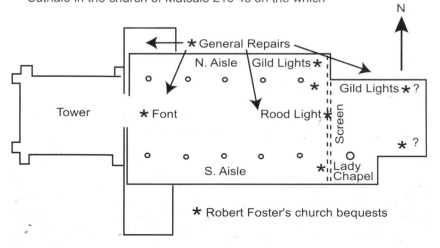

* Robert Foster's church bequests

I will have a gravestone laid to the price of 40*s*.

Finally a third theme, and one in Mattishall's later history, is the link between Mattishall and Parson Woodforde in the person of Mrs Bodham. She was a close friend of Parson Woodforde and he frequently joined her and her circle at South Green House, the nearest thing to a manor house in Mattishall. Mrs Bodham was born Anne Donne and married the Reverend Thomas Bodham who died in 1796; she lived for another 50 years and died aged 98. Woodforde refers on many occasions to his visits. For example, on 29th July 1783

> About 1 o'clock I took a ride to Mattishall to Mr. Bodhams and there dined and spent the Afternoon with him, Mrs. Bodham, Mr. and Mrs. Ball of Catfield, Sister to Mrs. Bodham, Mrs. Davy, Mr. Smith, Mr. and Mrs. Howes, Mr. Ashull and Nancy. – We had for Dinner, a Piece of boiled Beef, some Beans and Bacon, a couple of Ducks rosted, a Veal Pye and some Apricot Dumplins. At Quadrille this Evening won £0. 2. 0. As we were coming away Mrs. Howes came to me and asked me to their House it being their Rotation next, but I entirely refused to go, as they had not only kept away from mine very lately, but would not let Miss House come who was very desirous of coming to Weston. I gave it to her, and most of the Company seemed pleased with my behaviour. We did not get home till after 9 in the Evening. Nancy was obliged to change Horses, the flies teazing Phyllis very much which made her kick a little.[6]

In such wonderful little excerpts a light is cast on 'Mattishall society' in 1783, on eating habits and on problems of transport for even short distances – Weston Longville is only four and a half miles from Mattishall. Oxford University comes into the picture because Woodforde held the living of Weston Longville from Magdalen College which was given it by Sir John Fastolf.

The two ancient universities link Mattishall with the outside world; the wool broggers linked it with the Suffolk and European cloth trades; and Parson Woodforde, because he kept a careful diary, takes us back to the Mattishall area in the late 18th century.

The Rise of Tudor Yeomen: *Cawston*

Cawston lay in the hundred of South Erpingham and with Aylsham it was one of the two largest settlements of the hundred. Why the hundreds of North and South Erpingham bore the name of a relatively unimportant Norfolk parish is not clear. Sandred has suggested that perhaps it was the name for the place of the followers of Eorp.[1] Erpingham as a place-name occurs in 1044–7[2] before those of either Cawston or Aylsham but Sandred points out that in 1222 the Patent Rolls referred to 'the hundred of Cawston', meaning South Erpingham. Blomefield noted that a hundred court was held at Cawston in 1226.[3] As the map shows, the two Erpingham hundreds occupied a large area of north-east Norfolk. All Norfolk's hundreds existed by 1066 and were used by the Normans as their administrative units in the Domesday survey in 1086. Some of them, including the Erpinghams, may represent folk areas reaching back to well before 1066.[4]

By 1086 Cawston was an important royal manor with a population of about 685 and a value of £40 compared with its royal neighbour of Aylsham with

The hundreds of north-east Norfolk

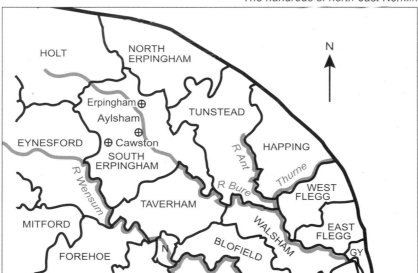

a population of about 695 and a value of £25. By 1332 the lay subsidy gave Cawston as having 106 people paying tax (making a population of about 450) at a value of £11 10s 3d compared with Aylsham's 81 taxpayers (or a population of about 360) paying £13 0s 2½d.[5] Cawston had a market by 1263 and two fairs and a sheep fair. It was an important market town firmly

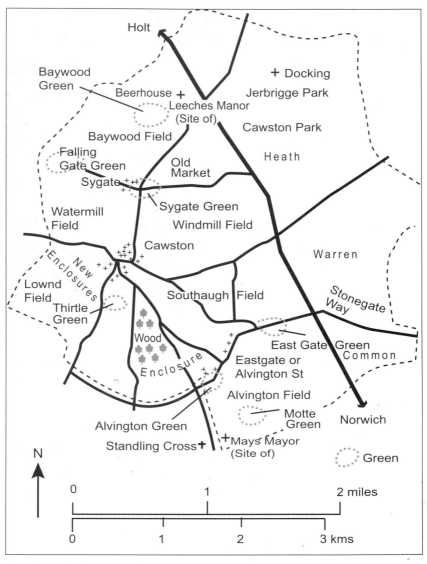

Cawston c.1600.

sited within what had become by 1346 the worsted weaving area of the county.[6] Sutton points out that Queen Isabella, wife of Edward II, granted the ulnage (quality control of the cloth) to Robert Poley in 1326 and that she held Cawston manor. Cawston was benefitting from being in royal hands.

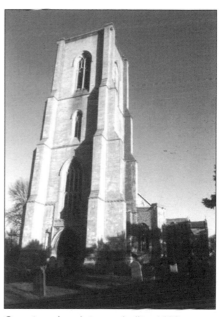

With royal patrons it is not surprising that Cawston gained in another way. Michael de la Pole, Earl of Suffolk, was Lord of the Manor by grant from the Crown in 1385 and he died in 1414. The rebuilding of Cawston church is attributed to him and his successors.[7] The tower, replacing an earlier one that fell in 1412, was faced with Caen stone and was a lavish gift to the parish. The inhabitants also, benefitting from the prosperity of the cloth industry, contributed to this rebuilding of the church; for example, John Thornham gave 20s to the tower in 1421.[8]

The wills left by members of a community are priceless sources when perhaps all else we know of

Cawston church tower, built c.1400.

them are sporadic entries in the manor court records. Their inventories too are valuable but, sadly, though 67 Cawston wills have survived from 1300 to 1600 the associated inventories have not. The early wills often specify bequests in kind as well as those in cash. In 1503 , when Robert Machion died,[9] he left 3s to the high altar of St Agnes and 6s 8d to the repair of the church; he also left money to the four gilds (St John the Baptist, St Agnes, St Peter and the Trinity). Further bequests were made to the light of St James and to the plough light of 'Saygate' and for seven trentals (masses) to be sung for him. Here we see, as in most pre-Reformation wills, the intimate relationship of a parishioner to his church, the gilds being their burial and social clubs.

In a transcription of Cawston church goods for 1552 there is a list of the possessions of 'Our Ladies Gylde there': 24 platters weighing 27*lb* 8*oz*, 23 dishes, 24 saucers, 4 latten basins, 4 spits, 2 latten candlesticks, 3 tablecloths, 3 towels, one gown, valued at £1 18s. This picture of the equipment used by a gild on its feast days gives a feel of the social occasions celebrated before the Reformation. It is not clear that Cawston ever had a gild house or hall, as compared with Wymondham which had several.[10] The sad note, after this list and that of other church regalia which were sold, is 'that only the chalice and the great bell are used in divine service'.[11] At Long Melford, a lavishly furnished church, the plate and vestments were delivered to the Crown Commissioners in 1553 and the church was allowed to retain only two chalices and a lectern.[12]

Another will, that of Katherine Goodman made in 1513, makes an interesting bequest to Alvington 'dawnce' (dance) and also to the ploughlight of the same street.[13] This makes it clear that what is now known as Eastgate was then known as Alvington but the dance would seem to have been performed there; was the light also in a small shrine there as well? In other words, did the religious festivals of Cawston stretch out to the edges of the parish? Katherine left small bequests to the Greyfriars and Whitefriars in Norwich and to the other orders of friars there. She left 3d to each house of lepers in Norwich. Do these bequests, as in other Cawston wills, reflect links with Norwich by birth or by trade? Henry Goodman, in 1526, in requesting a priest to sing for his soul, notes: 'if my son Richard hereafter be opprest I woll he shall sing the oon year at Cambridge if he woll and the other year in Cawston'.[14] This reference suggests that Henry's son was studying at Cambridge so we can see how Cawston yeomen had connections with a larger region.

Curiously no castle or manor house survives that gives a clue as to the

Beerhouse Farm: a possible manor site according to Blomefield and Rye.

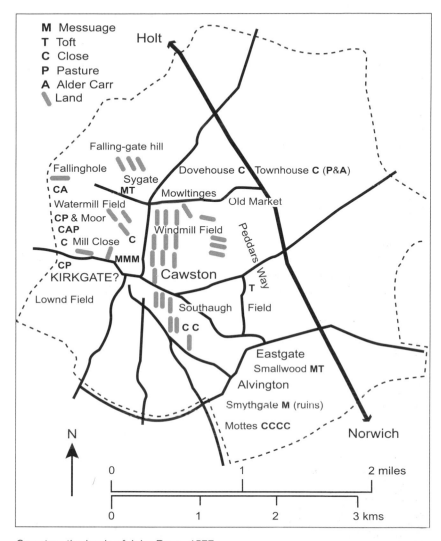

M Messuage
T Toft
C Close
P Pasture
A Alder Carr
**** Land

Holt

Falling-gate hill

Fallinghole

Sygate

CA   **MT**

Watermill Field

CP & Moor

CAP

C Mill Close   **C**

MMM

CP

KIRKGATE?

Lownd Field

Dovehouse **C**   Townhouse **C (P&A)**

Mowltinges

Old Market

Windmill Field

Peddars Way

Cawston

T

Southaugh   Field

C C

Eastgate

Smallwood **MT**

Alvington

Smythgate **M** (ruins)

Mottes **CCCC**

Norwich

N

0   1   2 miles

0   1   2   3 kms

Cawston: the lands of John Reve, 1577.

grandeur of former owners of Cawston from the de la Poles to Queen Elizabeth I. Blomefield and Rye both suggest it was on the site of Beerhouse Farm. Slight documentary clues in manorial admissions suggest the site of the manor as being between the High Street and New Street. In 1582/83 Ralph Gray and his wife, Agnes, before the steward gave to Edward Hammond and Richard Gyles

> one tenement built and two roods of land of the cite of the Manor of Cawston lying between the tenement formerly of Richard Rayny . . . to the east and the tenement and orchard formerly of Edward Hauchyns now Simon Blome on the west and abuts on the street called New Street and on the Queen's highway north.[15]

Other pieces of land are also located as 'of the cite of the manor'.

It is perhaps because Cawston was a royal manor (until it was sold by James I to the Hobart family in 1610) that it has a fine surviving archive relating to manor records, to disputes between the Crown's 'farmers' and the inhabitants and to the church. Amongst these records are several out-standing maps. Cawston, in some ways, fitted the model of the medieval village open-field layout. The settlement was surrounded by four open fields (or more, depending on how the information is interpreted). The map of Cawston Manor shows Watermill or West Field, Windmill Field, South-awe or Woodgate Field and Lownd Field. It also shows Baywood Field to the north of the inner system and Alvington Field to the south. The almost classic medieval layout was modified by the existence of two subsidiary settlements, Southgate (Sygate) to the north and Eastgate (Alvington) to the south-east of Cawston. Whether Baywood and Alvington Fields were related to the subsidiary settlements is at present an open question.

That this was a period of rapid change in the land ownership of Cawston, as it was in many other East Anglian parishes, is clear when we look at the details of this map.[16] Many enclosures are shown and the dating of these is given prior to about 1600. From the 1550s a number of tenants whose names occur more than once have 'taken' closes out of the open fields. The map was presumably drawn in order to clarify where things had got to, perhaps at the request of Queen Elizabeth's officers after she inherited Cawston from her mother, Anne Boleyn.

Two examples of the way in which lands were distributed are illustrated by first returning to Robert Machion in 1502 and then looking at John Reve's lands in 1574. Robert Machion included his possessions in his will and gives some idea of a Cawston yeoman's possessions at the beginning of the century. He left his wife Margaret two little yards called Sprotts Yards and five acres (two hectares) of copyholds as well as his house with three acres enclosed. When acreages are specified as opposed to the phrase 'my lands' we have a clue as to the scale of an individual's property. The terms 'enclosed' and 'lands' suggest he held a croft plus strips. He then

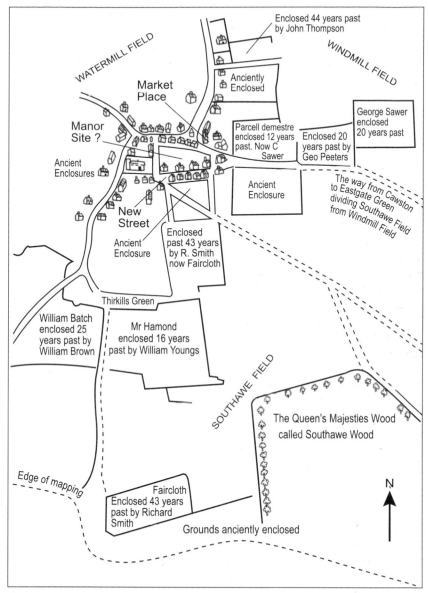

Enclosed 44 years past
by John Thompson

WATERMILL FIELD

WINDMILL FIELD

Market
Place

Anciently
Enclosed

George Sawer
enclosed
20 years past

Manor
Site ?

Parcell demestre
enclosed 12 years
past. Now C
Sawer

Enclosed 20
years past by
Geo Peeters

Ancient
Enclosures

The way from Cawston
to Eastgate Green
dividing Southawe Field
from Windmill Field

Ancient
Enclosure

New
Street

Ancient
Enclosure

Enclosed
past 43 years
by R. Smith
now Faircloth

Thirkills Green

William Batch
enclosed 25
years past by
William Brown

Mr Hamond
enclosed 16 years
past by William Youngs

SOUTHAWE FIELD

The Queen's Majesties Wood
called Southawe Wood

Edge of mapping

N

Faircloth
Enclosed 43 years
past by Richard
Smith

Grounds anciently enclosed

Cawston c.1600, from a map of the manor in the Norfolk Record Office [4521E].

went on to leave Margaret 'six mother sheep called ewes with five lambs'. She was also to receive his 'horse, a mare, the cart, the plough with the harness thereunto belonging and all the barley that is sown on the said lands'. Then, perhaps with feeling for the state of the road when he carted his barley, he left 6s 8d for the 'repair of the highway at the Watering and in Segate'. As an afterthought, his god-daughter Agnes was to have his pewter pot with the long neck.

Robert would also have had grazing rights on one, or some, of the commons of Cawston on which he is most likely to have run some sheep. He would also have cut gorse, smallwood and heather and had the right to dig for gravel on the common. He was not one of the most prosperous yeomen but he held land to pass on to his wife and he left her stock and grain. It was barley that was in the barn, not oats or rye or wheat; barley had the highest value because of its use in brewing. In 1574 John Reve, a tenant of the manor, died and a full inventory of his lands was made.[17] His lands were divided into 51 strips in the common fields totalling 56½ acres (average one acre a strip), 14 closes with four tofts, totalling 33 acres averaging 2½ acres. John's lands were spread through the open fields, although he did have closes taken out of the open fields. His other closes were meadows on the west side of the parish (see the map on page 107).

Wills, inventories and manorial records tell us about the more prosperous people in the community. It is always more difficult to find something about the less fortunate. From 1540, instead of leaving money to the religious gilds people began to specify bequests to the poor. In 1559 Stephen Parson, a worsted weaver, specified that 'Jane, my wyfe, shall give unto the pore people at my buriall day one dozen bread and a ferkin bere'.[18] Ralph Stanhawe, Gent., said in his will in 1581: 'Item I give unto the pore people of Cawston 10s. Item I give unto the pore of Brandiston fyve shillings'.[19] Such bequests were sporadic but by the 1560s the Tudors put the responsibility for looking after their poor firmly on the parish. In 1572 they created the posts of overseers of the poor and in 1597 they allowed them to levy a poor rate. It is against this background that Cawston's excellent surviving records, especially those kept by George Sawer between about 1580 and 1610, throw much light on the poor of the parish.

A document entitled 'Orders to be observed by the Overseers of the Poore within the Towne of Cawston' makes the overseers each responsible for a proportion of the poor households within the parish.[20] It then goes on with ten orders, the first of which states 'that consideration be presently had what stock will be necessarie in the towne in flax, wooll and hempe for setting such poore at worke as want other employment and that a rate be presently made of money collected for providing of the same'. This underlines that the textile trades were still regarded as the best way of occupying the poor.

One of the parish papers provides some very interesting material as to 'the names of such as live by their hand labour with their children to be employed in worke in Alvington Street to Eastgate'.[21]

Seven householders are named as are 24 children aged from 18 years to six months. A column headed 'worke' follows the children's names and ages and it implies that the children were knitters, as those of Nicholas Dennis, or spinners, as the three children of Alice Patterson. The next column is headed 'by whom' and Nicholas and Alice are given as the employers. In the case of Fayth Starkon a Mr Sankey is the employer. So as well as having a street we find that at least seven houses existed inhabited with their families and that they lived by knitting and/or spinning. The spinners perhaps provided yarn for the householders to weave cloth as well as for knitting. We can, at least in part, people the street to which, nearly a hundred years earlier, widows were leaving money for 'lights' (placed in tabernacles perhaps) and for the 'dance'. Alvington in the 16th century must have echoed to the shouts of many children playing on their half acre of green amongst tethered cattle when they were not being held to their knitting and spinning.

Sawer and his colleagues listed all the properties in Cawston and in 1601 he listed the poor and their dependants over the age of 60; only four were men, the rest widows, and they totalled 37. A list of the poor over 40 totalled 170 (including families). These two lists total 207 poor.[22] Amussen noted another list in which Sawer divided Cawston into four groups, again in 1601; 68 households paid local rates, 20 households, with 56 members, did not contribute to rates but had either a house or a cow and 57 households paid no rates and had neither house nor cow and 22 households received parochial relief.[23] She argues that a polarisation of wealth took place in Cawston between 1574 and 1617. Kate Tiller draws attention to Spufford's work on three Cambridgeshire villages when the ratio of landless wage labourers changed from 2:5 in the 1520s to 3:5 in the 1690s.[24] Cawston was becoming more sharply divided between some 14 successful yeomen and an increasing proportion of the poor; perhaps this was in part a result of a shift of work within the textile industry towards Norwich.

Baptists and a waterway: *Worstead*

Worstead is, of course, best known for its assumed link with worsted cloth. It was one of the holdings of the Abbey of St Benet at Holm listed in Edward the Confessor's charter of 1046. There is no doubt that its two churches, both belonging to St Benet's, existed in 1066, but St Andrew's was abandoned in the sixteenth century.[1] The surviving church of St Mary is the focal point of the centre of the main settlement. St Benet's held many manors and churches in the Bure and Ant valleys, the main manor being that of North Walsham. Canute's founding of St Benet's in 1020 and the need to endow it with an income from surrounding lands shows that many settlements were already established by that date.

The parish of Worstead is 2,600 acres in area and it lies on the west bank of the River Ant, stretching inland on to the plateau; its northern and west-

The estates of St Benet at Holme in the Ant and Bure valleys c.1046.

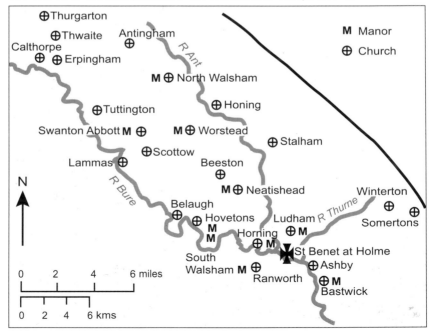

Church Plain, Worstead

ern boundaries are arbitrary and a small watercourse defines its southern boundary. Westwick, meaning the western dairy farm,[2] may perhaps be regarded as a later subdivision of the original Worstead vill and that does have a clearcut western boundary of Westwick Beck. That, in turn, abuts Swanton Abbot, a name reflecting the St Benet's ownership.

St Mary's church, Worstead, from the south.

The parish is unusual in its layout in that it has four hamlets: Briggate, Bengate, Lyngate and Withergate, all with the element *gate* in their name, meaning a street. The major settlement has a cluster of interesting flint and brick buildings around the small church plain to the east of the chancel of St Mary and to its south. These buildings are mainly of the 16th and 17th centuries and have replaced earlier weavers' and merchants' houses. Pevsner

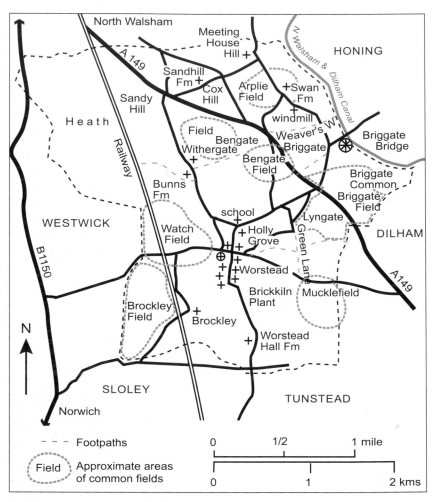

The parish of Worstead showing some medieval elements. (Source: B. M. S. Campell, 'The Extent and Layout of Common Fields in Eastern Norfolk' in Norfolk Archaeology *XXXVIII Part 1, Fig. 3, derived from a copy of a map of 1600 made by Robert Wymer in 1781 [Church Commissioners' map 11905]).*

and Wilson draw attention to several pieces of evidence to support the former weaving activities in three of these buildings.[3] The impact of a monastic house on the nature of settlement has already been discussed in the case of Binham. However, after the dissolution, King Henry VIII exchanged the lands of the Bishop of Norwich with the former lands of the Abbots of St Benet's. Worstead therefore came into the hands of the Dean and Chapter of the cathedral, its manorial and tithe records continued in institutional hands and this provides a priceless archive for those interested in following its history.

Maps are interesting both for their own sake and as sources for the study of the development of the landscape. As a result of the Dean and Chapter's inheritance of the manor and church of Worstead one or two valuable maps have survived. The Church Commissioners' map 11905 is a copy, redrawn in 1781, of an earlier map, and makes it possible to attempt a reconstruction of the approximate areas of the medieval open fields of Worstead. There were several of them – Worstead, unlike Cawston, was not a tidy 'typical' medieval village. This study does not attempt to explain this dispersal of the common fields but their names make one wonder if the separate hamlets, such as Briggate, each had their infields. Alternatively, as population expanded before the Black Death, new hamlets may have been created on the outer edge of the common fields in assarts (new enclosures) into the marginal woodland and heath of the parish (as happened at Cawston and Wacton). The fields, for convenience, would have borne the names of the new hamlets. Withergate does not appear to have grown around any obvious capital messuage; archaeological field work might throw more light on its age. The plan of the main settlement in about 1600 is much the same as the present village core, which still has a few outlying cottages to the north around a small green. Buildings appear to have been drawn conventionally and are shown by ten repeated shapes to the east of church plain. Several of these appear to date from well before 1781, perhaps as early as 1600; the undercroft would seem to be perhaps early-15th-century.

Undercroft under St Andrew's Cottage, Church Plain.

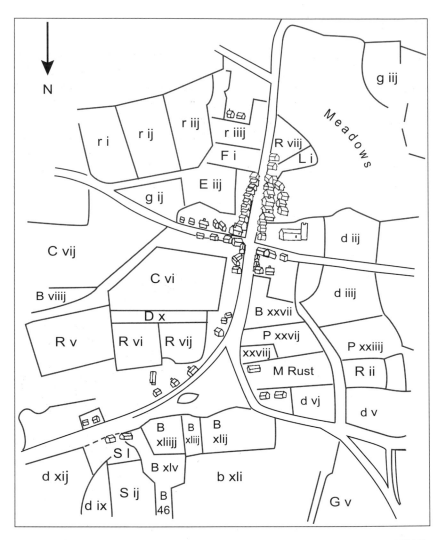

The village of Worstead c.1600 (derived from Church Commissioners' map 11905).

Despite the temptation to focus on the question of Worstead and the cloth named after it, the remainder of this account will concentrate on two later phases in the history of Worstead, the arrival of non-conformity and the development of the canal.

Meeting House Hill

Non-conformity has been strong in Norfolk; nearly every village had at least one chapel and many had two or three. Meeting House Hill is an isolated spot on the northern edge of the parish. This was a small settlement which grew around an attractive chapel built in 1829 for Particular Baptists. The census for religious worship for Norfolk 1851 shows that more Baptists worshipped there than did Anglicans in the parish church of St Mary.[4] There were, on average, 90 attending the Sunday School, as against 80 attending the one at the parish church. (The Primitive Methodist chapel was not built until 1892.) The Baptists had established a spread of chapels in East Norfolk by 1851; three earlier congregations were established by 1672 in North Walsham, East Ruston and Ingham.

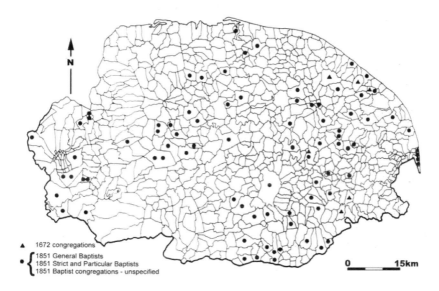

▲ 1672 congregations

● { 1851 General Baptists
1851 Strict and Particular Baptists
1851 Baptist congregations - unspecified

0   15km

Map showing the distribution of Baptist congregations in Norfolk, from N. Virgoe and T. Williamson (eds), Religious Dissent in East Anglia *(Norwich: UEA, 1993), p. 46.*

The Particular Baptists broke away, quite amicably, from the General Baptist Church of Smallburgh in 1717. Baptists chose baptism in adulthood when they could make a conscious decision to join their church. The 'particularness' was that they believed in predestination as elaborated by John Calvin (1509–64), believing that God had decided that if you were one of the chosen you would go to heaven. The Worstead Baptists established a church with 120 members. The graveyard of the chapel and its former site lie near that of the present chapel. A series of influential and much loved pastors made their contributions to the development of the chapel and its flock. Reverend Edward Trivett, for example, served as pastor for 52 years. It is recorded that he baptised over 400 and sent 11 young men out as pastors into 'God's Vineyard', a phrase often used in their records. They were especially fortunate that Reverend Richard Clark, a successful businessman, came from Devon; 'his property . . . placed him in a position of usefulness above most of his brethren'[5] and in 1829 he gave £250 to the new chapel and other bequests as well. There was even stabling for the horses of those who came some distance to services.

The non-conformist chapels faced a problem of adding to and maintaining their membership; like Congregationalists and Quakers, they placed strong emphasis upon the 'correct' behaviour of their members. Worstead Baptist Church, like so many other non-conformist groups, kept excellent records. Their church book for 1717–1826, the years of the first church, gives a flavour of the difficulties they faced in maintaining a satisfactory level of conformity in their flock.[6] An early record of 8th October 1729 reads:

It is agreed upon by the church meeting together in Worstead to withdraw commun-ion and fellowship from Phillip Harris late a member of this congregation for the following crimes that have justly been laid to his charge. First for his unlawful drinking, secondly for defrauding his neighbours by not paying them what is their due. Thirdly, for living unbecom-ing a Christian with

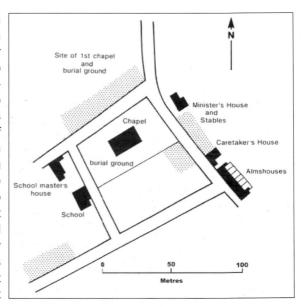

Meeting House Hill: plan showing the original chapel and the later developments around it. (From Janet Ede and others, Halls of Zion *(1994), p. 43.)*

his wife and fourthly, for rejecting the Christian and brotherly admonitions that have been given once again. Fifthly and lastly, for his going on and recovering in his Evill way.

Concern with maintenance of religious and social behaviour was an important aspect of chapel life but the caring side of the Baptist community also appears from the record. Those suffering misfortune were looked after, for example, by offering financial help:

Nov. 7, 9 and 16. Collected for the late Brother Farmery's widow and three children the sum of £11 19s.

Nov. 24. Previous to this day Brother Thomas Gibbs having exercised his gifts among us and by a majority was considered likely to be useful in the Lord's Vineyard this day preached from Acts 20 to 24 and was sent out to preach the everlasting gospel. J F Beard, Pastor.

This picture of discipline, of looking after their own and of widening their membership is typical, not only of the Baptists, but of other non-conformist denominations during this period across the country.

Meeting House Hill: New Baptist Chapel, built in 1829

The North Walsham and Dilham Canal

The mill at Briggate had existed for several centuries before the navigation. Domesday Book states that there was always (i.e. from 1066) one mill[7] and Sandred gives a reference to it in 1595.[8] It was the water-powered corn mill for the St Benet's manor which could only be located on the River Ant on the eastern boundary of the parish. The North Walsham and Dilham Canal bounded the parish of Worstead from Meeting House Hill via Briggate Mill to form the parish boundary, or nearly so, as far as Canal Farm.

Briggate, already a separate hamlet within the parish, was enlarged as a result of the construction of this short canal which ran from Antingham Ponds, north of North Walsham, to Dilham. The ancient parish boundary, which had been defined by the twisting course of the River Ant, was not followed exactly by the canal because the river was straightened in order to improve navigation. The Act 'for making a navigable canal from the rivers Ant and Bure, at or near Wayford Bridge, near Dilham to the towns of North

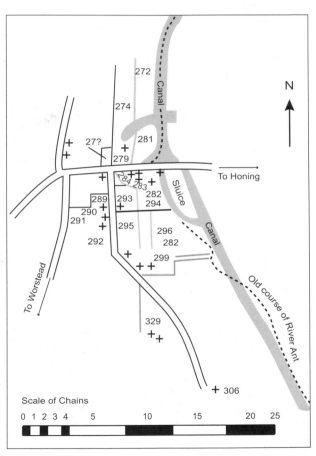

Briggate Mill and the North Walsham and Dilham Canal (map based on the Tithe Map of 1844 in the Norfolk Record Office [DN/TA 775]).

Above: *Briggate mill in 2002.* Below: *Derelict lock at Briggate on the North Walsham and Dilham Canal (built c.1812).*

Walsham and Antingham in the county of Norfolk' was passed in 1812. As had become the custom, plans for a proposed navigation had to be deposited with the Clerk to the Peace of Norfolk at the Shire Hall. A very nice copy of the Act was bound for the Treasurer who was no less than Richard Hanbury Gurney Esq.[9]

The Company could not stop people making canals on their own land to join it, though as far as is known no one did this. The 20 shareholders were empowered to raise £30,000 between them with borrowing powers for another £10,000. Another Act of 1866 altered this, allowing any number of shareholders who could do so to sell the canal provided that 'no sale or lease shall authorise the closing of the said canal'.[10] In 1907 the trustees of Mr Press, who bought it in 1866, sold it. In 1912 the Great Flood broke the lock gates and the canal was never reopened. By this date the railways had taken much of the canal's trade and its trading income in 1907 was only £400. A fine sale catalogue of 1907 had some excellent photographs of the then much less tree-lined canal course.

The canal's direct impact on the parish of Worstead was at Briggate Mill. A lock was built there and the ancient mill site had to be bypassed. The Act of 1811/12 specified that no mill should lose its head of water as a result of the making of the canal. Overall the farms and many small businesses along the canal benefitted from the easier movement of bricks, gravel, bone for the fertilizer mill at Antingham and coal.

The Great Flood of 1912 caused much damage in the Ant Valley and there was not enough capital to rebuild the narrow locks. A brief attempt, echoed later by the railway lines, had been made to improve communications for this rural area but first rail, then road transport finished it off. Whether the canal will be revived as an extension of the amenity waterways of Broadland remains to be seen.

An estate village: *Great Melton*

Great Melton lies six miles to the west of Norwich. It is a small parish with two churches in the same churchyard, one of which is in ruins. They lie to the east of an attractive park in which are the remains of the former hall. The parish has a small population and is well hedged and wooded. It is part of a large family estate of which the main hall is at Marlingford. Archaeology, a complicated story of two churches and the interrelated evolution of a park and new road system form the themes for this account.

In 1986/7 there was an exceptional find of an important Mesolithic site in Great Melton. The report by John Wymer and Peter Robins summarises the finds as follows:

The near total excavation of a concentration of flintwork on arable land at Great Melton has produced the first unselected collection of a Mesolithic industry in East Anglia, dug and recorded under controlled conditions. The setting of the site is unusual, being high above and a kilometre distant from the nearest river valleys of the Tiffey and the

The two churches at Great Melton

Yare. It is interpreted as a short-lived hunter's camp. The discarded artefacts below the ploughsoil were, for the most part, disturbed by rabbit burrows, but the distribution may still reflect something of the original shape of an assumed shelter. Typology indicates parallels with the prolific scatter of Mesolithic artefacts on Kelling Heath, but dating can only be judged by the similarity of the Great Melton industry to known Early Mesolithic industries elsewhere in southern Britain dated between 7000 and 8000 BC. A thermoluminiscence date on a burnt flint suggests it may be more recent.

The examples of axes illustrated were 17 cm and 15 cm in length. The amazing total of 743 tools and 31,074 other artefacts was collected from an excavated area of 107 m². Wymer and Robins suggest this might be the debris from a few days' stay by a hunting group. As no organic remains were found, pollen remains for example, the dating could only be by analogy with another site at Kelling Heath.[1]

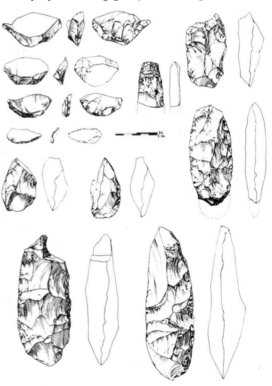

This summary shows that it is unusual to find such a site on the boulder clay plateau. It raises the question of whether, as more and more field-walking is carried out, further sites might be discovered on the boulder clay. Great Melton has, as is noted, a unique site but it is by no means unusual for Mesolithic flints to be found. This underlines that here, as in many other Norfolk parishes, there is evidence of some type of human activity having taken

Mesolithic axes/adzes (from J. Wymer and P. Robins, 'A Mesolithic Site in Great Melton' in Norfolk Archaeology *vol. XLII part II (1995), p. 139, fig. II).*

place for nearly 10,000 years. Man was beginning to change the post-glacial environment.

Jumping from these finds we can move to the impact of Rome which has left its mark in two ways in Melton. Caistor St Edmund was the centre of a pattern of roads and settlement during the Roman period. On the Hethersett/Melton parish boundary a Roman farmstead with tiled roofs, flint and mortar walls and using greyware pottery has left its mark on the land and heaps of flint walling have been pulled up by the plough.[2] Roman building materials were valuable to a non-brickmaking culture and the Anglo-Saxons plundered this site. The quoins of All Saints' Church were strengthened with Roman tile. Neither the Mesolithic nor the Roman finds have had any impact on the present map of Great Melton. What certainly did was the arrival of Saxon and then Norman invaders.

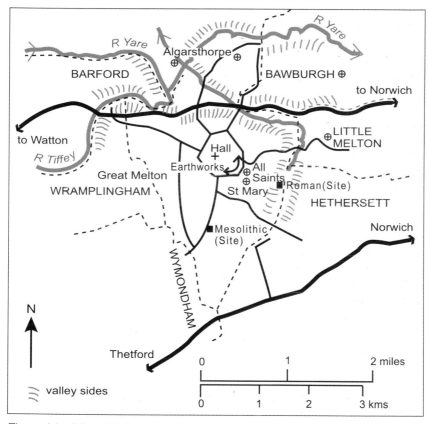

The parish of Great Melton.

Ladbrooke's drawing of Melton All Saints church.

All Saints' Church has evidence of Saxon work in its north wall. This and St Mary's Church resulted from the imposition by the Normans of a manorial system. St Mary's was the church for Hacon's Manor and All Saints' that for Peverell's Manor which took its name from Ralph Peverel, a Norman lord from whom Waring held it in 1086. Ketel, a Saxon thain, held it before 1066.[3] It is the story of these two churches that provides a second theme in this study of Great Melton. In 1822 and 1823 J. B. Ladbrooke drew the two churches from the same angle. Even these drawings conceal an earlier stage in their history when, in 1710, All Saints was declared redundant and the two livings were united, using St Mary's church.[4]

By Act of Court 1882:

> The rector and churchwardens of the said Parish of Melton Saint Mary and All Saints alleged that by an Act of Parliament passed in or about the year 1710 the Parishes of Melton Saint Mary and Melton All Saints were consolidated and made one Rectory and Parish and that by the authority of the same Act the Rector and Churchwardens of the said parishes so united were empowered to pull down the Parish Church of Melton All Saints and to apply the old material thereof from time to time towards repairing the Parish Church of Melton Saint Mary the said churches both in one churchyard.

Ladbrooke's drawing of Melton St Mary's church.

That the said Church of Saint Mary consisting of a chancel, nave, tower and a south porch does not afford sufficient accommodation for the inhabitants of the said parish and is also in a very bad state of repair.

That it is proposed to take down and dilapidate the same and to rebuild and restore the chancel nave tower and south porch of the

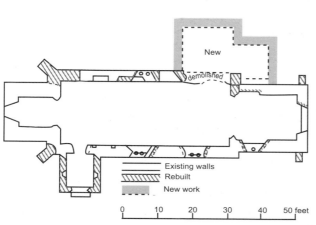

Plan of All Saints church, Great Melton, showing the works carried out in 1882 (from the Consistory Court papers DC/CON in the Norfolk Record Office, Acts of Court 1882).

Church of All Saints the walls of which are still standing and which is built on a firmer foundation and is of larger dimensions and of greater architectural beauty and better adapted for the parish church than the Church of Saint Mary and to erect a transept and vestry on the north side thereof. That the font bells monuments and such internal fittings as are sound and fit will be removed from the Church of St Mary and replaced in similar positions in the Church of All Saints.

Though All Saints had its fabric robbed in 1710 and was heavily rebuilt in 1882, there is evidence in its present fabric of Roman tiles in its eastern gable quoins, which may have come from the Roman site already mentioned. On its north side the nave near the tower has what appears to be a Saxon doorway edged with Roman tile and brick. On this evidence it seems possible that some of the fabric of All Saints may survive from the church which was mentioned in the Domesday entry of 1086.[5] The date of St Mary's Church is more difficult to assess but Ladbrooke's drawings suggest Early English windows, perhaps about 1300.

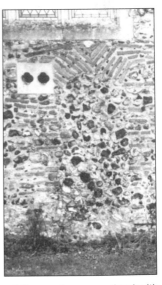

A third element in the changing face of Great Melton is that of the development of a park and of a new road system. As Cushion and Davison have shown, Great Melton Park has had a complex past.[6] Cushion's plan shows a former roadway cutting across the park and two areas of earthworks of which those immediately west of the two churches, as suggested by Davison, may be the site of Peverell's Manor before 1610.

A Saxon doorway edged with Roman tile at All Saints.

In 1567 John Downes of Great Melton left a very detailed will.[7] His first bequest was that his executors should provide a dinner 'immediately after my death for the inhabitants of Great Melton and 3s 4d to be distributed to the poor as judged appropriate'. He also gave 26s 8d to be divided amongst the poor people of Wramplingham, Carleton Forehoe, Barford, Marlingford, Colney, Cringleford, Hethersett and Little Melton. This suggests his estate must have been considerable although the amount is small! His will continues:

To Christian my wife after my death for her natural life shall have my copyhold messuage and mansion place the which I do dwell in in Great Melton which were sometime Henry Thetford's Gentleman together with all the orchards, gardyns and waters to the same belonging and also all the lands . . . pastures, meadows, wayes and feadings, wods and underwoods with all their appurtenances and com-modities to the same mansion house belonging . . . also one and a half acres the site of the manor which I purchased of my nephew Francis Downes.

Roman tile in the south-east quoin of the nave at All Saints.

The overall picture is of an already land-scaped estate with the various compo-nents specified. The reference to the site of the manor (Peverell's according to Blomefield[8]) as distinct from his mansion suggests that he had already laid out the first hall by the time of his death. The site then went to Thomas Anguish in 1609.[9]

Great Melton Park (from The Earthworks of Norfolk *in* East Anglian Archaeology 104 (2003), p. 215, fig. 140)

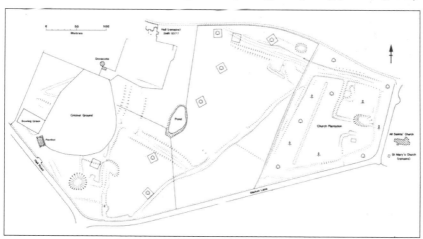

Great Melton Hall photographed before the fire of about 1900.

Anguish was a rising figure who became mayor of Norwich in 1611 and, according to Kelly's Directory, it was his family that built, or rebuilt, the hall then.[10] This date looks right for the E-shaped southern half of the hall as it was before the fire.

The effect of the fire of about 1900 was to produce a 'hollow' park with no house as its focal point. The park has survived and the former hall yards, complete with dovecote, are still there. The park has many mature trees in it and a screen of woodland round it survives as echoes of an earlier phase in the history of the parish.

*Great Melton park and (*inset) *the dovecote, survivals from the days when a great house stood in thepark.*

The 18th century was the period of the development of the gentleman's landscaped estate. The process began with the great houses of the nobility, such as that of the Hobarts at Blickling, and gradually filtered down until owners of smaller gentry houses and large rectories laid out their minor parks and large gardens in appropriate style. A screen of trees usually defined the new park, as it still does at Great Melton; exotic species such as cedars of Lebanon, holm oaks and later redwoods began to appear and lakes were dug or dammed to improve the vista, as for example at Wolterton. With the large parks, such as Holkham and Houghton in Norfolk, earlier villages were demolished and at Houghton the new village was built outside the main entrance gates. Earthworks remain in the parks showing the sites of the former villages.

The final touch to the creation of a new park was to ensure that 'the public' could not just wander through using the roads near to the new or extended mansion. The procedure for carrying out this clearance was formalised in the later 18th century. Proposals to change the line of a road had to be put to the Justices of the Peace and, rather like modern planning procedures, deposited with the Clerk to the Peace for the county. This was a fortunate move for the researcher and several volumes of Road Diversion Orders have survived in the Norfolk Record Office. The Justices had to ensure that an alternative and 'equally convenient' new route would be provided. The map of Great Melton shows the remains of the hall surrounded by a pentagon of roads and footpaths. Between 1777 and 1818 these formed a continuous new road skirting the park. The old roads within the park were closed in 1776 and the public no longer

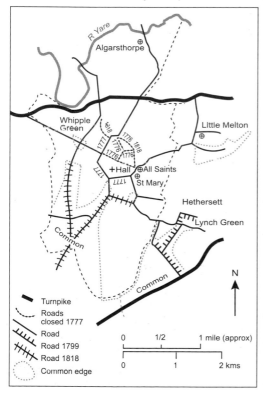

131

passed by the Hall.[11] In 1777 the new road was laid out around the park.[12] A second series of road changes also affected Melton and this came in 1818. The Parliamentary Enclosure Act for Great Melton was passed in that year, Hethersett had been enclosed in 1799 and Wymondham's massive enclosure award was in 1806. A large area of common 'waste' remained in Great Melton once land had been allotted under the award. The Evans-Lombe family used this Act to close part of the new road of 1776 round the park. Thus the creation of a park combined with the impact of an enclosure award redesigned the pattern of roads in the parish. This was by no means unusual and the majority of English parishes underwent at least some road closures and the laying out of new roads between 1770 and 1820. The acts, their resultant awards and the valuable maps associated with them relevant to Norfolk are all to be found in the Norfolk Record Office.

Above: *The south-west corner of the park with roads laid out in 1777 to the west and south round the park.*

Opposite, top: *The new road of 1777 to the south of the park.*

Opposite, bottom: *The distinctive shape of the park stands out in the general field pattern when viewed from the air. The photograph is taken looking west of north, with the two churches just off the picture to the right. Comparison can be made with the map on page 131.*

The impact of Norwich: *Hethersett*

Hethersett is a large village lying on the boulder clay plateau four miles to the south-west of Norwich. It was the capital manor of the hundred of Humbleyard, a name, sadly, that only survives as that of a rural deanery and of a licensing district. It was lost as an administrative name when Forehoe and Henstead Rural District was created in 1888 because it was the middle hundred of the new district and it was not revived when administrative imagination, and perhaps historical ignorance, cast all hundredal names aside and thought up South Norfolk as a safe bet. Hethersett is a place most people go round on what is now the A11. Yet there are over 5,000 people living in what has become a large satellite village of Norwich.

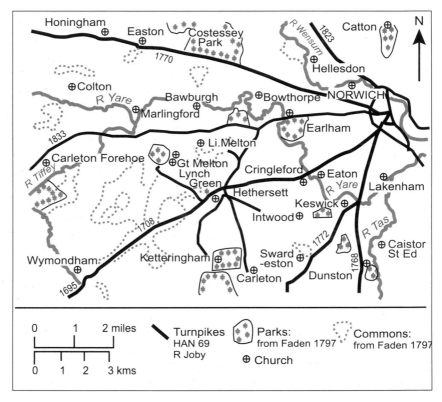

Hethersett was divided into, or had overlapping into it, several manors. It had no religious house in it and no obvious manorial sites that survive as standing buildings or earthworks. The manors were those of Hethersett Hacons, Hethersett Cromwells and Hethersett Woodhall. There is a little evidence, south of Church Farm, that a manor site may have existed there; a moated site survives at Thickthorn but it was not the site of a manor house and Hethersett Hacons had a manor house in Great Melton. The focus of the late medieval village lay between the parish church of St Remigius and a junction from the main Norwich to Thetford Road leading to the Meltons, from which a ring of crofts lay around Lynch Green. The church was marginal to the main settlement but perhaps related to the possible manor site to the south of it.

As in so many other Norfolk villages this complex pattern of manors meant that many tenants held lands from two or more; in Foxfield, for example, a tenant might hold three neighbouring strips of land, each from a different manor, with slightly different conditions of tenancy.

A number of medieval arable fields lay around the village. The shallow west-to-east valley had, and still has, damp meadow land along it; it is joined by a small stream from the plateau to the south of Church Farm. South-east of Hethersett lay the small parish of Cantley, merged with Hethersett in 1393.[1] A large farmhouse is its sole survivor and across the road from it the humps and bumps of the church site can still be seen.

Hethersett, like many other villages within a day's travel of Norwich, became a desirable place in which those who had made money in Norwich came to live. *The Mayors of Norwich 1403 to 1835* lists seven Norwich mayors as residing in Hethersett by the time of their death.[2] Many other mayors owned some property in Hethersett, such as Thomas Layer, mayor in 1576, 1585 and 1595. Roger Ramsey, mayor in 1610, and Roger Bene, mayor in 1710, both owned the Thickthorn Estate, the nearest part of the parish to Norwich. Other mayoral houses were the Old Hall, Hethersett Hall, Hill House and Wood Hall, in periods ranging from 1785 to 1933. Of these Thickthorn Hall, Old Hall and Wood Hall were earlier buildings. Hill House was built by the Brown family (John Brown was mayor in 1798). Hethersett Hall was built by John Luke Iselin about 1770; he was a wool stapler. It then came into the hands of the Back family of whom Thomas Back had been mayor in 1809.[3] Later members of the family laid out the obligatory gentleman's park with an ornamental lake from which footpaths were diverted. The Hill House estate and, a little earlier, the Rectory estate had fine ornamental trees planted in them so that these now provide a wooded vista for the commuter returning home from Norwich.

The main theme of this village study is that of movement; the road to Thetford and on to London, has been a very important influence in determining how the village has evolved. The road from Norwich to Thetford is an old one: the first source of information about our post-Roman roads, the Gough map of about 1330,[4] shows the road from Norwich to London as running via Bury St Edmunds and Cambridge. It was the road also followed by Celia Fiennes from Norwich in 1680 when she commented on the causeway from Wymondham to Attleborough and noted the women spinners sitting under the hedgerow by the road.[5] John Ogilby, in his *Britannia*, published in 1675, showed on his linear map Hethersett Common stretching for three miles, Woodhall at the west end of the village and the church at the east end with a large wood to the south of the road at Thickthorn. The road was well established but the weight of traffic on it led to demands for improvement and in 1695/6 the first Norfolk turnpike was created between Wymondham and Attleborough; in 1708 this was extended to Hethersett. The heavy clay soils of the plateau made winter travel difficult until at Larling they gave way to the sandier soils of the Breck. Further Acts in 1726 and 1746 added to the powers given to the trustees to deal with the state of the road between

The King's Head, one of three inns on the turnpike.

Hethersett and Fettlebridge at Attleborough. An Act of 1767 appointed Justices of the Peace for the county as trustees for the turnpike. They had the power to erect gates for toll collection, to acquire land for gravel or for road straightening and to draw on parishes for labour on the road. Capital was raised by investors taking out shares and then expecting to receive a dividend.

A list of tolls set in 1839 for Cringleford gate emphasises that narrow wheels were regarded as more damaging to road surfaces: for 'every cart drawn by two or three horses (with wheels of less breadth than four and a half inches) 4½d. The same with wheels of six inches or more in breadth drawn by not more than four horses 3d.'[6]

Not everyone had to pay; those going to vote in parliamentary elections were exempt, as were all clergy when travelling on their business. Gate-keepers must have had many arguments when deciding on who was exempt. The tollgates were let out; the tollkeeper Charles Cooper, for example, paid the trustees at Cringleford £416 4s 6d in 1787. It was then up to him to make a greater sum than this.[7]

Whitegates, a gentry house on the turnpike, later to become the control centre for the county fire brigade.

The minute book gives a list of small modifications approved by the trustees for the improvement of the road: gravel pits were needed for surface materials for the road, difficult bends needed straightening and streams bridging. Four items from the minutes show how the turnpike was gradually

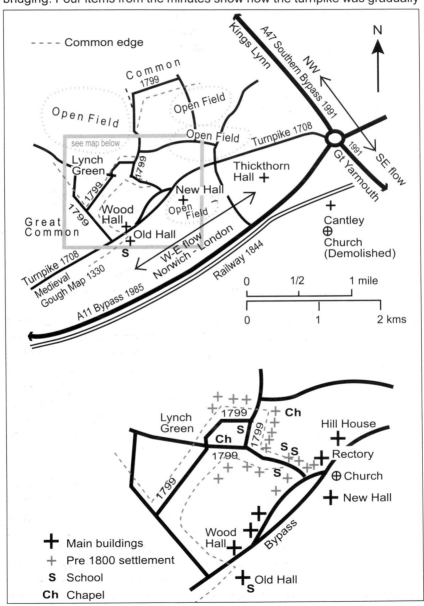

improved in and around Hethersett and remind us that roads were being changed before the days of by-passes.

15 October 1790
Ordered that the turnpike road be carried in a strait line from Besthorpe corner over the Common in the parishes of Besthorpe and Attleborough agreeable to the plan produced before us.

15 April 1795
Ordered that Mrs Bates be paid for her gravel pits at Hethersett in occupation of Mr Reynolds being 43 rods at 3s 9d – £7 17s 6d.

3 November 1821
(Contract with G. S. Kett, executor of Mr Back)
Removal of a barn and also such a portion of land adjoining as would enable them to widen and improve that part of the Turnpike Road at the foot of the hill near the Water Lane in the Parish of Hethersett.

22 April 1822
Minute that Mr Brown be thanked for his help during the progress of the work of improvement on the turnpike in the Parish of Hethersett.

The efforts to maintain a major road never keep up with the demands on it and Hethersett illustrates this well. The parish church, three inns and several good houses lined the turnpike. In 1963 the first step at bypassing the settlement was made but by the late 1980s this had proved insufficient and the new Wymondham/Hethersett bypass on the A11 was completed. In 1991 this linked with the South Norwich bypass, part of the improved A47. The ancient junction of two routes meeting at Tombland in central Norwich was replaced by the Thickthorn roundabout which in turn has changed the western edge of Norwich and will do so even more in the years to come.

The maps show that the great common of Wymondham and Hethersett extended well within the parish boundary and a long tongue reached into the parish to be surrounded by some of the earliest surviving buildings in it; this was called Lynch Green. The enclosure award of 1798 led to the enclosing and allotting of the former common land. New straight access roads were laid out along the eastern edge of the Great Common and across Lynch Green. The building that gradually took place thereafter has completely filled in the former Lynch Green. Enclosure has therefore added a new pattern of subsidiary roads additional to the major road that has already been discussed.

Church, Chapel and School

The parish church dominated the religious life in Hethersett in the 18th century, partly because it had a long-serving rector, John Berney, appointed in 1736, who rebuilt the rectory in the middle of the century and remained in post until 1782. He was a pluralist, holding also the two rectories of Saxlingham and that of St Clement at the Bridge in Norwich; he became Archdeacon of Norwich and was chaplain to the bishop. He was a member of the gentry Berney family of Reedham and he spent a great deal of his own money on the restoration of the rectory. He was a man of some status in the church and in the parish. The picture of the diocese as a whole was very different and under Bishop Bathurst it was known as 'the Dead See'.

As has been pointed out in the section on the Baptists of Worstead, nonconformity developed rapidly in Norfolk and across the country from the mid-17th century onwards. Hethersett never had an early Independent church; that in Wymondham, founded in 1715, was the nearest as was the Friends' Meeting House of 1687. The well-documented Wiffen family of Hethersett[8] did hold a licence for Quaker meetings from 1737 in one of the earliest surviving timber-framed houses in the village. The Methodists also used a private house in 1792 and the first licence for a Wesleyan chapel was given in 1817. By 1833 a Primitive Methodist group was also using the Great Melton Road chapel.[9]

Myrtle Cottage, where Quakers used to meet.

In the 1851 religious census over 100 Wesleyan Methodists and about 15 Primitive Methodists were recorded. Importantly, the Wesleyan Methodists recorded fifty Sunday School scholars.[10] In 1898 a Baptist Chapel was opened on Henstead Road. Roman Catholics attend a church in Wymondham and, as in so many places, the ecumenical movement has led to Methodists, Anglicans and Catholics having joint services – a long way from the diversification that took place between 1600 and 1900.

Religious differences have had a very strong influence on the way in which schools have evolved and as the non-conformist churches began to found first Sunday Schools and a little later, village schools, so the Church of England began to respond. In Hethersett a small Anglican school was founded in 1817; this was largely thanks to benefactors, two of whom were clergy. This underlines how the early development of church schools depended on local interest. It was of course to be 1871 before many parishes gained a school but in 1861 a second building was erected in Hethersett with a grant from the National Society for Promoting Religious Education. Farm labourers' children were to pay 1d a week, farmers' children 6d.[11]

So much for churchgoers, but a local landowner, Edward Lombe of Great Melton Hall, made a start with a British School; Caroline Lindley continued the work and a second school for 'liberal and unsectarian education' was built after 1850. The National and British Schools were separate until 1954. The growth of Hethersett has been paralleled by the full sequence of First, Middle and High Schools; will the full age range of up to eighteen ever

Hethersett Methodist Chapel.

develop? In addition, the Old Hall is now a private boarding and day school for girls from four to 18.

The gradual expansion of Norwich, the use of bus and car and access by a main route has led to Hethersett becoming a commuter village. Interestingly, the building of the railway and the station in 1845 had no effect on the growth of the village. Yet the rapid growth after World War 2 was followed by the provision of two new schools, a branch library and a bank, since lost. The key determinant in major development was the provision of a new main sewer in the 1980s. The parish church is now less isolated than it must have been since about 1300. The 'gentry' houses, built or added to by Norwich mayors and aldermen, have now become a residential home, a private girls' school, the county fire service HQ, the residence of the Vice-Chancellor of the university and luxury flats. The intersection of the A47 and A11 will lead to more growth but it has already spawned a petrol station and Little Chef. Hethersett, like other villages near major English cities, has grown fast. More careful thought might have led to a conscious village centre having been created but only new town status or single ownership of a site, as at New Hunstanton, seems to have allowed such long-term planning to take place in England.

Hethersett Old Rectory.

References

Note: References in square brackets are to documents held in the Norfolk Record Office.

Hunstanton

1. C. H. Luton Brain, 'The Icknield Way' in *Norfolk Archaeology* XXXIII Part IV (1965), map opposite p. 418.
2. Tony Gregory and David Gurney, *Excavations at Thornham, Warham, Wighton and Caistor St. Edmund, Norfolk,* East Anglian Archaeology report 30 (Gressenhall: Norfolk Archaeological Unit, 1986), map on p. 2.
3. J. Wymer, 'Early Iron Age Pottery in Hunstanton' in *Norfolk Archaeology* XXXIX Part III (1986), pp. 286–96.
4. R. P. Sawyer, 'Anglo-Saxon Charters' in *Transactions of the Royal Historical Society* no. 1489, p. 417.
5. Bailiffs' accounts for Hunstanton and Mystrells Manors, 1605–26 [LEST R9].
6. *A Dragge of the Sea Lawres of Hunstanton* [LEST BH1].
7. Cord Oestmann, *Lordship and Community: The Lestrange Family and the Village of Hunstanton, Norfolk, in the First Half of the Sixteenth Century* (Woodbridge: Boydell Press; Norwich: University of East Anglia Centre for East Anglian Studies, 1994), p. 125.

8. [LEST R9, 1605, p. 27].
9. Walter Rye, *Norfolk Families* (Norwich: Goose, 1911–13), vol. 1, p. 481.
10. [LEST P6].
11. [LEST P6].
12. [LEST P6, 1610].
13. Will of Edward Spencer, 1532 [NCC 67–9 Platfoote].
14. *A Plan of the Proposed Village of Hunstanton St Edmunds* [PRA 678, 383X2].

The Terringtons

1. R. J. Silvester, *The Fenland Project, 3: Marshland and the Nar Valley, Norfolk*, East Anglian Archaeology report 45 (Gressenhall: Norfolk Archaeological Unit, 1988), p. 156.
2. A. Rogerson and R. J. Silvester, 'Middle Saxon Occupation at Hay Green, Terrington St Clement' in *Norfolk Archaeology* XXXIX Part 3, pp. 320–22.
3. Rogerson and Silvester, p. 40.
4. 'The Red Hills of Essex' in Colchester Archaeological Group *Bulletin* 30 (1990).
5. Edward Miller, *The Abbey and Bishopric of Ely: The Social History of an Ecclesiastical Estate from the Tenth Century to the Early Fourteenth Century* (Cambridge: Cambridge University Press, 1951), pp. 77, 83.
6. Alan Crosby, *A History of Cheshire* (Chichester: Phillimore, 1996), pp. 70–71.
7. Terrington St Clement glebe terrier 1716 [DN/TER].
8. C. Barringer, 'A History of Sheepfarming from Saxon Times until AD 1600' in *East Anglian Studies* 2 (Open University, 1991).
9. Will of Richard Cooper, 1584 [NCC 315 Bate] and inventory [INV 2 no. 11].
10. *Faden's Map of Norfolk* (Guist: Larks Press, 1989). Introduction by J. C. Barringer.
11. Silvester, p. 41.
12. Miller, p. 96, quoting Min Accounts 1132/10, 13.
13. Survey of the Manor of Terrington, 1650 [NRS 1123, 10B3].
14. Terrington Town Book, 1655–1757 [1 Sotheby 30/4/71, R153B].
15. *Orders for Stinting the Commons and with what Cattle and what Time* (no date) [NRS 8046, 24 B 2]
16. Ridging = ridgel: an immature ram. I. H. Adams, *Agrarian Landscape*

Terms (IBG Special Publication 9, 1976), p. 143.
17. [BL 38/8].
18. David Dymond, *The Norfolk Landscape* (London: Hodder & Stoughton, 1985), p. 124.
19. D. P. Mortlock and C. V. Roberts, *The Popular Guide to Norfolk Churches,* vol. 3 (Cambridge: Acorn, 1985), p. 130.
20. A copy of the Act is in the Norfolk Heritage Collection in the library in Norwich. I am grateful to Dr Clive Wilkins-Jones for providing me with a copy.

Weeting

1. W. G. Clarke, *In Breckland Wilds* (R. Scott, 1926).
2. Mark Bailey, *A Marginal Economy? East Anglian Breckland in the Later Middle Ages* (Cambridge: Cambridge University Press, 1989).
3. Barbara Green, *Grime's Graves, Norfolk* (London: English Heritage, 1993).
4. [NRS 21393 Cab 1 (1760)].
5. [MS 13469, 40C5 (copy), 1541–2].
6. [NRS 13489, 40C6].
7. Neil Batcock, *The Ruined and Disused Churches of Norfolk*, East Anglian Archaeology report 51 (Gressenhall: Norfolk Archaeological Unit, 1991).
8. [NRS 13489, 40C6].
9. [MC 491/1, 749x9].
10. [NRS MS 13736, 40 EZ].

Hickling

1. Barbara Cornford, 'The Sea Breach Commission in East Norfolk 1609–1743' in *Norfolk Archaeology* XXXVII (1979), pp. 137–45.
2. Blomefield, vol. IX, p. 303.
3. [NRS 1986 II BI].
4. C. T. Smith in J. M. Lambert, J. M. Jennings and others, *The Making of the Broads: A Reconsideration of their Origin in the Light of New Evidence,* Royal Geographical Society Research series, 3 (London: John Murray, 1960).
5. Tom Williamson, *The Norfolk Broads* (Manchester: Manchester University Press, 1997), p. 98.

6. [DN/MSC/6/6].
7. S. J. Noel Henderson, *The Story of Hickling Priory 1185–1536*.
8. Copy of extract of Augmentation Office and Chancery Proceedings James I, bundle S25 no. 38 [NRS MS 21191, 165X2].

Brampton and Burgh-next-Aylsham

1. Thomas Browne, *Concerning some Urnes Found in Brampton Field* (1667).
2. Christopher Sparey Green, *Excavations in the Roman Kiln Field at Brampton, 1973–4*, East Anglian Archaeology report 5 (Gressenhall: Norfolk Arcaheological Unit, 1977).
3. Green, p. 92.
4. Green, p. 93.
5. Margaret Gelling, *Place-names in the Landscape* (London: Dent, 1984), p. 265.
6. Nikolaus Pevsner and Bill Wilson, *Norfolk 1: Norwich and North-East*, The Buildings of England series (London: Penguin, 1997), p. 417.
7. Tom Mollard, *Millgate, Aylsham: A Study by the Local History Research Group* (Aylsham: Aylsham Local History Society, 1993).

Bawburgh

1. Peter Wade-Martins (ed.), *An Historical Atlas of Norfolk* (Norwich: Norfolk Museums Service in association with the Federation of Norfolk Historical and Archaeological Organisations, 1993; 2nd ed. 1994).
2. Carol Twinch, *In Search of St. Walstan: East Anglia's Enduring Legend* (Norwich: Media Associates, 1995).
3. Twinch, p. 29.
4. Twinch, p. 106.
5. H. W. Saunders, *An Introduction to the Obedientiary and Manor Rolls of Norwich Cathedral Priory* (Norwich: Jarrold, 1930).
6. [DCN 52/4 Fo 43].
7. Will of Thomas Harvey, yeoman, 1601 [NCC 119 Gardyner].
8. Inventory of Thomas Harvey, yeoman [NCC Inv 17.89, MFX/6].

The Shoteshams

1. *Domesday Book* vol. 33 parts 1 and 2, *Norfolk* edited by Philippa Brown (Chichester: Phillimore, 1984).
2. Peter Wade-Martins (ed.), *An Historical Atlas of Norfolk* (Norwich: Norfolk Museums Service in association with the Federation of Norfolk Historical and Archaeological Organisations, 1993; 2nd ed. 1994), sections 13, 14 and 15.
3. Margaret Gelling, *Place-names in the Landscape* (London: Dent, 1984), pp. 15, 16, 29, 31.
4. Thanks to Alan Davison for drawing my attention to this suggestion in A. H. Smith, *English Place-Name Elements,* vol. 2, English Place-Name Society Publications vol. 26 (Cambridge: Cambridge University Press, 1956), p. 115.
5. *St. Benet of Holme, 1020–1210: The Eleventh and Twelfth Century Sections of Cott. MS. Galba E. ii.: The Register of the Abbey of St. Benet of Holme*, transcribed by J. R. West, Norfolk Record Society Publications vols. 2 and 3 (Fakenham and London, 1932), p. 3.
6. *The Register of the Abbey of St. Benet of Holme,* p. 100.
7. D. Smith, 'Report of the Deserted Medieval Village of Shotesham St Mary' in *Gwynedd Journal* (1969), p. 172.
8. R. Morris, *Churches in the Landscape* (London: Dent, 1989), p. 163.
9. W. J. Goode, *Round Tower Churches of South East England* (Norwich: Round Tower Churches Society, 1994), p. 110.
10. Nikolaus Pevsner and Bill Wilson, *Norfolk 2: North-west and South*, The Buildings of England series (London: Penguin, 1999), p. 344.
11. Tom Williamson, *Origins of Norfolk* (Manchester: Manchester University Press, 1993), and also in *An Historical Atlas of Norfolk* (Norwich: Norfolk Museums Service in association with the Federation of Norfolk Historical and Archaeological Organisations, 1993; 2nd ed. 1994), pp. 40–43.
12. Timothy L. M. Hawes, *The Inhabitants of Norfolk in the Fourteenth Century: The Lay Subsidies 1327 and 1332*, Norfolk Historical Aids 20 (Norwich: the author, 2000), pp. 241–3.
13. *The Register of William Bateman, Bishop of Norwich 1344–1355* edited by Phyllis E. Pobst, vols. 84, 90 (Boydell Press for the Canterbury and York Society, 2000).
14. Brian Cushion and Alan Davison, *Earthworks of Norfolk,* East Anglian Archaeology report no. 104 (Norwich: Norfolk Museums and Archaeology Service, 2003), p. 67 and fig. 44.
15. D. Smith, p. 174.

16. I. S. Leadam, 'The Inquisition of 1517' in *Transactions of the Royal Historical Society,* new series, vols. 6, 7 (1892–3).
17. D. Smith, p. 182.
18. *The Registrum Vagum of Anthony Harison* transcribed by Thomas F. Barton, Norfolk Record Society Publications vol. 32 (Norwich: Norfolk Record Society, 1963), p. 65.
19. Blomefield, vol. 5, p. 519.

Wacton

1. Tom Williamson, *The Origins of Norfolk* (Manchester: Manchester University Press, 1993), pp. 24–8, fig. 2.1.
2. O. Schram, 'Place Names' in *Norwich and its Region* (Norwich: British Association for the Advancement of Science Norwich Local Executive Committee, 1961), p. 143.
3. George Munford, *An Analysis of the Domesday Book of the County of Norfolk* (London: J. R. Smith, 1858), p. 20.
4. S. Addington in *Norfolk Research Committee Bulletin* 24 (1980).
5. 'The Norwich Taxation of 1254' in *Norfolk Archaeology* 17 (1910), pp. 46-158.
6. Survey of 1602. *East Anglian Notes and Queries I* (1866).
7. L. McMurdo, 'Wacton Common' in *Norfolk Research Committee Bulletin* 24 (1980). This section draws heavily on this article.
8. Wacton Churchwarden's Accounts 1699–1715 [PD 496/64].
9. Wacton Overseers' Accounts 1673–83 [PD 496/78].
10. C. Barringer, B. Cornford and Alan Davison in *Norfolk Research Committee Bulletin* 18 (1977).
11. M. Rodgers, transcribed from Survey of Wacton 1541 [PD 496/105], p. 4.
12. W. G. Hoskins, *The Making of the English Landscape* (London: Hodder & Stoughton, 1955), p. 120.
13. Geoffrey I. Kelly, *Wacton Hall: A History* (1988).
14. Will of John Sherman of Wacton, 1597 [NCC 47 Eade], transcribed by Geoffrey Kelly.
15. Alan Carter, 'Survey of Wacton Hall', manuscript, April 1988, cited by Geoffrey Kelly.
16. Inventory of George Raynes [NCC Inv/9/311].

Binham

1. Binham Court Book, 1625, transcribed by Birstall [NRS 24072, 108X5], Court 2.
2. *The Victoria History of the County of Norfolk* vol. 2 (London: Constable, 1906), pp. 343–6.
3. George Munford, *An Analysis of the Domesday Book of the County of Norfolk* (London: J. R. Smith, 1858).
4. Nikolaus Pevsner and Bill Wilson, *Norfolk 1: Norwich and North-East*, The Buildings of England series (London: Penguin, 1997), p. 389.
5. *The Victoria History of the County of Norfolk*, vol. 2, p. 343.
6. Map of Binham, 1792 [MS 4925 BRA].
7. Birstall Cartulary MS Cotton Claudius D13 BM: English paraphrase by M. Kett [MC 619/1, 782X6]. Also Birstall Court Rolls [NRS 24072, 108X5].
8. Map of Binham, 1792 [MS 4925 BRA].
9. E. B. Birstall's Binham Papers on Enclosure [NRS 24075, 108X5].

The Mattishalls

1. J. and J. A. Venn, *Alumni Cantabrigiensis* (Cambridge: Cambridge University Press, 1922–7).
2. Roger Virgoe, 'The Priory Estates' in *Norwich Cathedral: Church, City and Diocese, 1096–1996* edited by Ian Atherton and others (London: Hambledon Press,1996), p. 355.
3. *The Register of Thetford Priory* edited by David Dymond, Part 2, *1518–1540,* Norfolk Record Society Publications LX (Norwich: Norfolk Record Society; Oxford: Oxford University Press for the British Academy, 1996), p. 551.
4. William Hudson and John Cottingham Tingey, *The Records of the City of Norwich* vol. 2 (Norwich: Jarrold, 1910), p. 181, cccxxxiii.
5. K. Allison, *The Wool Supply and the Worsted Cloth Industry in Norfolk in the 16th and 17th Centuries*, PhD thesis, Leeds University, 1956.
6. James Woodforde, *A Country Parson: James Woodforde's Diary 1759–1802* (London: Century, 1985), p. 82.

Cawston

1. Karl Inge Sandred, *The Place-names of Norfolk, Part 3:The Hundreds*

of North and South Erpingham and Holt (English Place-Name Society, 2002), p. 80.

2. P. Sawyer, 'Anglo Saxon Charters' in *Transactions of the Royal Historical Society* 1055 (1988).
3. Blomefield, vol. VI, p. 240.
4. C. Barringer, 'Norfolk Hundreds' in Peter Wade-Martins (ed.), *An Historical Atlas of Norfolk* (Norwich: Norfolk Museums Service in association with the Federation of Norfolk Historical and Archaeological Organisations, 1993; 2nd ed. 1994), p. 88.
5. Timothy L. M. Hawes, *The Inhabitants of Norfolk in the Fourteenth Century: The Lay Subsidies 1327 and 1332*, Norfolk Historical Aids 14 (Norwich: the author, 2000).
6. A. Sutton, 'The Early Linen and Worsted Industry of Norfolk' in *Norfolk Archaeology* XL, pp. 201–5.
7. Nikolaus Pevsner and Bill Wilson, *Norfolk 1: Norwich and North-East*, The Buildings of England series (London: Penguin, 1997), p. 429.
8. S. Cotton and P. Cattermole, 'Medieval Parish Church Building in Norfolk' in *Norfolk Archaeology* XXXVIII, part 3, pp. 235–79.
9. Will of Robert Machion [NCC 418 Popy, MF4].
10. Brenda Garrard, *Wymondham Parish Gilds in the Early Sixteenth Century* (Wymondham: Reeve, 2003), pp. 13, 14.
11. Cawston Parish Manuscripts [PD 193/31].
12. David Dymond and Clive Paine, *The Spoil of Melford Church: The Reformation in a Suffolk Parish* (Salient Press, 1989), p. 54.
13. Will of Katherine Goodman, 1513 [NCC 69 Coppinger, MF37].
14. Will of Henry Goodman, 1526 [NCC 103–4 Heywarde, MF39].
15. Admission of Edward and Richard Gyles of Edward Hammond and Richard Gyles, 25 Eliz. [NRS 24811, 134X6].
16. These changes are discussed by Bruce M. S. Campbell in 'The Extent and Layout of Common Fields in East Norfolk' in *Norfolk Archaeology* XXXVIII (1983), pp. 5–32.
17. Terrier of the lands of John Reve, 1577 [NRS 27216, 361X3].
18. Will of Stephen Parson, 1559 [NCC 174 Colman, MF55].
19. Will of Ralph Stanhawe, 1581 [NCC 349 Moyes, MF65].
20. [P186D].
21. [MC 148/15, 624X8].
22. List of the poor in Cawston, 1601 [NRS 2604, 12B2].
23. S. Amussen, *An Ordered Society* (New York: Columbia University Press, 1988), p. 17.
24. Kate Tiller, *English Local History* (Stroud: Sutton, 1992), p. 124.

Worstead

1. Neil Batcock, *The Ruined and Disused Churches of Norfolk*, East Anglian Archaeology report 51 (Dereham: Norfolk Archaeological Unit, 1991), p. 55.
2. Karl Inge Sandred, *The Place-names of Norfolk, Part 2:The Hundreds of East and West Flegg, Happing and Tunstead* (Nottingham: English Place-Name Society, 1996), p. 200.
3. Nikolaus Pevsner and Bill Wilson, *Norfolk 1: Norwich and North-East*, The Buildings of England series (London: Penguin, 1997), p. 736.
4. *Religious Worship in Norfolk: The 1851 Census of Accommodation and Attendance at Worship*, edited by Janet Ede and Norma Virgoe, Norfolk Record Society Publications 62 (Norfolk Record Society, 1998).
5. *A Manual of the Baptist Church at Worstead, Norfolk* (Norwich, 1859). A copy is item 20 in a volume of nonconformist pamphlets in the Colman collection at the Norfolk Heritage Centre local history collection in the library in Norwich.
6. Worstead Baptist Church Book 1717–1816 [FC 42/1].
7. Domesday Book 2.17.43.
8. Karl Inge Sandred, *The Place-names of Norfolk, Part 2:The Hundreds of East and West Flegg, Happing and Tunstead* (Nottingham: English Place-Name Society, 1996), p.160.
9. North Walsham and Dilham Canal Act 1811–12 [MC 20551/1, 906X7].
10. An Act to Amend the Act 1866 [BR 208/7/1].

Great Melton

1. R. J. Wymer and P. Robins, 'A Mesolithic Site in Great Melton' in *Norfolk Archaeology* XLII:2 (1995), pp. 125–47.
2. C. Barringer. Fieldwalking, Heritage Environmental Record 9270.
3. Blomefield, vol. V, p. 12.
4. Kelly's Directory 1888, p. 441.
5. *Domesday Book* vol. 33 part 2, *Norfolk* edited by Philippa Brown (Chichester: Phillimore, 1984), 32.4.
6. Brian Cushion and Alan Davison, *Earthworks in Norfolk,* East Anglian Archaeology report no. 104 (Norwich: Norfolk Museums and Archaeology Service, 2003), pp. 213–15 and fig. 4.
7. Will of J. Downes, 1567 [NCC 244 Folklin, MF59].
8. Blomefield, vol. V, p. 12.

9. Blomefield, vol. V., p. 12.
10. Kelly's Directory, 1888.
11. Road Diversion Order, 1776 [Road Order Box 1, no. 9].
12. Road Diversion Order, 1777 [Road Order Box 1, no. 17].

Hethersett

1. Blomefield, vol. 5, p. 33.
2. Basil Cozens-Hardy and Ernest Kent, *The Mayors of Norwich 1403 to 1835, being Biographical Notes on the Mayors of the Old Corporation* (Norwich: Jarrold, 1938).
3. *Hethersett Heritage* (Hethersett Society, 1999).
4. H. C. Darby, *An Historical Geography of England Before 1800* (Cambridge: Cambridge University Press, 1951), p. 260.
5. *The Journeys of Celia Fiennes* edited and with an introduction by Christopher Morris (London: Cresset Press, 1947).
6. Norwich–Thetford Turnpike List of Tolls [T3/19].
7. Norwich and Thetford Turnpike Minute Book 1, 2nd June 1787 [T3].
8. D. Arnell, *History of Myrtle Cottage, Lynch Green, Hethersett, Norfolk* (1994).
9. Hethersett Society Research Group, *The Book of Hethersett, a Norfolk Village* (Halsgrove, 2002).
10. *Religious Worship in Norfolk: The 1851 Census of Accommodation and Attendance at Worship*, edited by Janet Ede and Norma Virgoe, Norfolk Record Society Publications 62 (Norfolk Record Society, 1998).
11. *The Book of Hethersett,* p. 54.

Reading list

The literature of landscape history and village studies has grown hugely in the past twenty years. The titles selected all have supportive reading lists.

General texts

Peter Fowler, *Farming in the First Millennium AD: British Agriculture between Julius Caesar and William the Conqueror* (Cambridge: Cambridge University Press, 2002)

Mark Overton, *Agricultural Revolution in England: the Transformation of the Agrarian Economy, 1500–1850* (Cambridge: Cambridge University Press, 2002)

Oliver Rackham, *The History of the Countryside* (London: Dent, 1986)

Brian K. Roberts, *The Making of the English Village: a Study in Historical Geography* (Harlow: Longman Scientific & Technical, 1987)

Christopher Taylor, *Village and Farmstead: a History of Rural Settlement in England* (London: George Philip, 1983)

Tom Williamson, *Shaping Medieval Landscapes: Settlement, Society, Environment* (Macclesfield: Windgather Press, 2004)

Norfolk texts

F. Blomefield, *An Essay towards a Topographical History of the County of Norfolk* continued by C. Parkin, 11 vols (London, 1805–10)

Bryant's Map of Norfolk 1826 ed. J. C. Barringer (Guist: Larks Press, 1998)

Elizabeth Darroch and Barry Taylor (ed.), *A Bibliography of Norfolk History,* 2 vols (Norwich: University of East Anglia Centre of East Anglian Studies, 1975, 1988)

Domesday Book vol. 33, parts 1 & 2, *Norfolk* edited by Philippa Brown (Chichester: Phillimore, 1984)

David Dymond, *The Norfolk Landscape* (London: Hodder & Stoughton, 1985)

Faden's Map of Norfolk 1797 ed. J. C. Barringer (Guist: Larks Press, 1989)

Nature in Norfolk (Norwich: Norfolk Wildlife Trust, 1977)

Nikolaus Pevsner and Bill Wilson, *Norfolk*, The Buildings of England series, 2 vols (London: Penguin, 1997, 1999)

Peter Wade-Martins (ed.), *An Historical Atlas of Norfolk* (Norwich: Norfolk Museums Service in association with the Federation of Norfolk Historical and Archaeological Organisations, 1993; 2nd ed. 1994)

Susanna Wade Martins, *A History of Norfolk,* Darwen County History series, (Chichester: Phillimore, 1984)

Susanna Wade Martins, *Norfolk: a Changing Countryside 1780–1914* (Chichester: Phillimore, 1988)

The current list of titles in the Norfolk Origins series is given on page 2.

Index